Harmonise with Life

A guide for finding your own path to inner peace, joy and love.

Tycho Photiou

Printed in Great Britain by
St Edmundsbury Press Ltd, Bury St Edmunds, Suffolk.

There are many quotations included within this book. They are the words of wise men and women through the centuries, up to, and including, the present day. Many of the quotations are from various religious texts, particularly Buddhism and Christianity.

Some of the relatively modern sources are acknowledged in the bibliography. Whilst the publisher has made every effort to obtain permission for the quotations wherever appropriate, this may not have been possible in every case. We would therefore like to thank everyone who contributed to provide the wonderful and rich teachings that you will find within these pages, and accept our apologies if any modern sources have not been adequately acknowledged.

Where there is no attribution given to the quotations, they are the authors own.

Dedication

*I would like to dedicate this book to
my late parents for giving me life and for
always allowing me to be myself, while giving me
gentle encouragement and support.
I deeply appreciate being born into
their gentle and loving hands.*

Acknowledgements:

When I completed the penultimate manuscript for this book, I gave it to 4 people, who I greatly respect, for proof-reading. I was impressed by the variety of feedback that I received. Although very varied, it was all extremely useful.

I would first like to thank Thomas Allen for his useful advice on various parts of this book and for his contribution to many of the quotations included in this book.

Thanks also to Lisa Ceneri for all her useful questions and comments.

I received some extremely useful feedback from the scientist David A. Chalmers especially on the section *The power of consciousness*.

The great sage Nolan John also gave me some very useful feedback on the entire book. Due to his wonderful sense of humour and through many of our conversations on the importance of laughter, the final section of this book came into being.

I would also like to thank my very wise sister Andrea for writing the preface to all my books and for always being ready to listen to my ideas and give me useful feedback whenever I have needed it.

All children are born equal but when they
arrive at the door of adulthood each
is measured by their capacity
to love their fellow man.
ANDREA PHOTIOU

Contents

Preface

Andrea Photiou

One of the finest gifts a human being can claim is the ability to change and adapt. This powerful human quality is so often overlooked that it is hard to measure its full potential. The environment we are born into, with its restrictions and expectations, can misguide and limit us as we are swept along on its conventional tides, making choices only within the constrains of the choices it offers - often feeling discontent and unfulfilled. Strangely enough for all our impressive technological advancement, we have still managed somehow to have lost our way.

Why is it that for so many people life seems to be one long struggle? Could it be because we have become so separated from our inner wisdom and instead taken on board the many limiting untruths that we are constantly bombarded with?

Have you noticed that the very things that have set the human animal apart from our brothers and sisters - the need to know, the need to develop, the need to create - seem to be the very things that have actually disconnected us from our real nature. Yet these are also the human qualities that will eventually return us to the place we naturally belong in this vast cosmic jigsaw puzzle.

This book is simply a presentation of another way, a series of signposts on an alternative path that removes the boundaries that society puts upon our choices, and hence breaking us free of limitation.

You will learn a way to explore, access and release your incredible human potential. This book is not advocating opting out of our social structure, nor side-stepping day to day

3

responsibility. Nor is it recommending compromising one's principles or sense of commitment - it more advocates how to live freely as an individual within the current structure of society.

This may seem like a contradiction but it isn't. Many of the restrictions we encounter are actually of our own making and so this book teaches a way to change your mental construct of the world, a way of seeing the world in a totally different light. It explains that you are the creator of your world, in fact, you are your world, and so if you want your life to be perfect, the way is simple - just be perfect.

> *All your suffering is rooted in one error.*
> *You believe that you live in the world,*
> *when in fact the world lives in you.*
> *ANONYMOUS*

Within these pages you will learn how it is separation and disconnectedness that creates loneliness and frustration - not just separation from people but disconnection from your true self. You will learn the importance of disattachment from that which limits and constrains you, maintaining your sense of separation. You will discover that it is only when you establish a connection with your true self that you will attain freedom.

This book is a challenge to the conventional attitudes we have developed as a race and adapted to as individuals. You will discover an alternative route - almost uprooting some of your most accepted beliefs, and, if you like, being presented, for your consideration, a new packet of seeds. Seeds gathered from the flowers of perception, imagination, logic, spirituality, natural instinct, emotion, insight, human experience and connectedness. And using that wonderful human gift of change and adaptability you can begin to blossom in your true colours.

4

The mystery
of life

MAPS AND MODELS OF REALITY

If our aim in life is to discover "truth" or to know reality, it is essential to ask ourselves whether such a possibility exists. We need to ask ourselves the question "Can we ever know reality itself?" This is a big question and I suspect that the answer is *yes*, but not through the rational mind, this deals only with symbolic or visual maps and models of reality that the mind constructs. Most scientists are aware of this when referring to say atoms or molecules. It is generally accepted by any *good* scientist that we can never really *know* what an atom is, we can only build up a mental model of an atom which hopefully, as we work on it, comes closer and closer to the actual reality that the model is representing - however it is important to keep in mind that all we can know on an intellectual level is the model and not the real thing. I believe that all we can "know" and discuss about any aspect of reality are simply words, symbols, maps and models. I emphasised the word "know" because most knowing within our culture refers to the accumulation of facts and the manipulation of those facts through the intellect. I believe that true knowing goes far beyond this - true knowing is a perception of the truth without the necessity of our normal perceptual apparatus. Our physical senses are extremely useful tools to help us interact with our environment, but to truly know something we have to make a stronger connection which transcends the senses. I believe that we can only make direct contact with reality through a religious or spiritual experience and not through intellectualising or scientific investigation.

So, all the words and symbols that we use to describe our ideas, beliefs and concepts, are just devices that our mind uses to help us to think and talk about our world. Words are essential for us to be able to communicate our thoughts, feelings and ideas about life, but we must realise that the words we use are just encoded symbols for our thoughts and feelings, and our concepts about reality are just maps of reality and not the actual reality itself.

There are difficulties in talking about many abstract concepts such as the soul, God or even love, as well as communicating to others the content of spiritual experiences such as momentary enlightenment or the near death experience. These difficulties arise due to the fact that when we want to talk about such things we need to use words, we need to label things - and this labelling is part of the problem, because as soon as we label something, what we are talking about is the label and not the thing itself.

Let me illustrate this point with an analogy. Let's suppose that you want to get to know London really well and so you buy several detailed maps showing various features of London and you sit in your room and study them for several months until you know every street and building in London. It is clear (I hope!) that in this situation you would still not really know London at all, you would only know the map of London. You could talk about London as if you knew it and whoever you talk to may say "This person really knows London well!", and in a way this is true even if you have never visited the actual territory. This is very similar to a scientist talking about the molecular structure of materials, he may sound like he *knows* what he is talking about but really he is just well familiar with his model. **But the Model is not the real thing!**

Now, you may say "If you interact with London itself instead of just looking at maps of it then you will *really* get to know it". I suggest that this is not the case and that you can never really *know* London, (in fact this statement has no real meaning). All that happens as you interact with London more is that you develop your mental model of it so that you feel that you know it better even though all that is really happening is that you are improving the mental model that you have constructed in your mind. In a similar way most scientific theories are not absolute truths but models that help us to get closer to understanding and explaining what is going on in the world.

The map is not the territory.
ALFRED KORZYBSKI

It is also very important to consider the fact that many so-called scientific theories are actually "red-herrings" which have the effect of distracting us from the truth rather than taking us closer to it. Once we think we know the truth we may stop searching elsewhere, but this is a big mistake since our "truth" may simply be a false dogma or a faulty model which may create the attitude "since I know the answer I no longer need to investigate".

So, is it possible to ever "know" the truth in the deepest sense of the word? Well, there are two very different levels of knowingness - the intellectual level and the experiential level. Within our current culture intellectual knowledge is the more highly respected of the two but throughout history especially in the East, the knowledge most relied on to awaken us has been that obtained through direct experience such as meditation or shamanic journeying. Shamans believe that the level of reality experienced while in an altered state of consciousness (such as dreams) is the true reality, while this three dimensional level is the illusory reality.

*The only way we can truly know reality
is to experience it.*

If a very wise, enlightened man were to directly *experience* exactly "what I am" and obtain all the answers to mankind's questions, then as soon as he tried to communicate it to anyone else, there would be limitations due to the language that he must use to verbalise the experience.

8

Despite the difficulties in talking about spiritual matters, if someone is open to what they are hearing, they will understand or relate to it, not on an intellectual level, but on an intuitive level. Within this book I will discuss many spiritual concepts such as Soul, God, Life, etc. If you can remain open minded and endeavour to connect with the words on an intuitive level, then I hope you may be inspired and move towards a deeper level of understanding of mankind and our place within this strange and mysterious universe.

In our quest for truth most of the masters throughout the ages have said that there is no more important question to consider than "What am I?" So, let us now address this very important question.

KNOW THYSELF

To be curious of that which is not my concern,
while I am in ignorance of my own self,
would be ridiculous.
PLATO

The journey towards self-discovery is the most important step that we can take if we are on the spiritual path. To "know thyself" is the most essential factor for the journey towards heightened awareness and wisdom.

Knowing others is knowledge,
Knowing oneself is wisdom.
THE BUDDHA

A few examples of questions that I will be considering are the following: Are we the observers of our mind, or is the mind observing itself? Is the subconscious a set of instructions within the brain that determines our working or is it a deeper part of the mind? Do we think from our brain or is the source of consciousness an energy field which the brain tunes into like a television receiver tunes into a transmitter? Can you have consciousness without thought? Can you have thought without consciousness?

Maybe it is possible that we haven't got a subconscious or a soul, but these concepts can give us a way of understanding and discussing what we are, in a much more useful way than the belief (as taught by many biologists) that we are simply a bundle of chemicals controlled by a fixed programme coded into our DNA.

> *Self-reflection is the school of wisdom.*
> *BALTASAR GRACIAN*

The model of understanding mankind that has been predominantly used in recent years is that we are a mind within a body, and that the mind is a product of the biochemistry of the brain. In this dualistic model, the mind is given incredible importance and is considered to be, among other things, the source of thought, the consciousness, the subconscious, the ego, the memories, the intellect, the personality and also the source of creativity. What I find more incredible is that this "concept" is given the location of the head. It is essential that we let go of this model since holding to it produces very severe limitations.

What most people attach to as being the "I" is the ego. This is the part of us that we may hope continues after the death of our physical bodies. The ego is the sum total of our likes and dislikes, our personality, our beliefs, our dreams and so on. But the ego is not what we are.

> *A person who knows himself as spirit never loses sight of*
> *the experiencer in the midst of experience.*
> *DR DEEPAK CHOPRA*

We are essentially spiritual in nature, but our mind is not our spirit. The soul, or self, or essence, is the observer of everything around us - it is the true site of perception. Language is again a problem here, because the simple term "my soul" implies that the soul is something that I have or own, as opposed to something that I am. If I have a soul then what is the "I" that has it?

> *I haven't got a soul,*
> *I am a soul.*

If man is essentially spiritual in nature then why do we have a physical body? One possible answer is that we have a body in order to provide us with a medium of two-way interaction so that we can have the experiences that are required for the development of the soul.

> *The body is the sheath of the soul.*
> *JUDAISM*

When I was a small child and up until I was in my early teens, I had the view that "I am my mind" and my body is a vehicle for my mind. This is the dualistic cartesian view that we have all been subtly indoctrinated to believe since the seventeenth century. This view changed one day while I was meditating and I *experienced* that **I am not my mind, I am the observer of my mind** - in fact, I am the observer of *all* my experience. Our essence, that part of us which is pure awareness, is observing the thoughts and images which pass through the mind, so, in a way, the mind is part of "the vehicle".

> *We are not human beings having a spiritual experience,*
> *we are spiritual beings having a human experience,*
> *WAYNE DYER*

We can become much more easy-going about life's difficulties and challenges if we can see everything that goes on as just **part**

11

of a play that we are observing, even what goes on in our own minds is just part of the performance.

To become the spectator of one's life
is to escape the suffering of life.
OSCAR WILDE

When we see a tree it is our awareness or essence that perceives it. If we think about what we are observing then we are using the mind to think about the object under observation, but the mind itself does not observe. Your mind is a tool that is linked to your consciousness, but it is not the source of consciousness. For this reason I do not like to use the term *conscious* mind since the mind itself is not aware or conscious. It is terminology like this which holds mankind back in his understanding of what we are. As soon as we ask a question such as: "What is the conscious mind" the question is assuming that the mind itself is conscious, and so the difficulty in answering the question might be, not so much because it is deeply profound, but more because it is an intrinsically invalid question.

Not only is the mind not conscious, but it is a distracter of consciousness. Imagine you are sitting peacefully by a mountain observing the breathtaking landscape, feeling connected and wonderfully relaxed. Your consciousness is now in the process of observation and no thought need be involved. In fact as soon as thought does become involved it detracts from the experience - if you start thinking "I should do this more often" or "I wonder why I don't always feel like this", or any other analytical thought then the beauty of the experience will vanish.

Too much analysis causes paralysis.
PROVERB

May spiritual sages say that our mind is actually the problem and

12

that to become closer to our true essence **we need to become not mindfully conscious but consciously mindless.**

If you can stop thinking for one moment you will go through the most tremendous experience there is - that you are the totality of this universe in your beingness.
LESTER LEVENSON

I would now like to discuss the distinction between mind and brain. I am using the simple definition of mind here as *that which thinks*, and not as *that which is conscious*.

First let us consider the question "Where is the mind?" Does this question have validity? Does the mind have a location? Within our culture the mind is given its location within the brain, indeed some people use the words mind and brain synonymously, however I see this as a result of the mechanistic world view which is the main doctrine of our western culture. Just as thought and consciousness should not be used interchangeably neither should mind and brain.

Although it is generally "believed" that we think from our brain, it is important to be aware that there is no evidence of this. I emphasise the word "believe" here, because many see this not as a belief but as an unquestionable truth, whereas it is actually only an assumption. It is true that thoughts are associated with neural activities but this by no means proves that neural activity gives rise to thought, in fact, the reverse could be the case, in other words it might be that thoughts may give rise to neural activity and not vice versa. Of course, on one level we know that both are the case since we have both sensory neurones which take impulses to the brain and stimulate a thought, and we have motor neurones which take thoughts and convert them to impulses. However, what I am saying here goes further than this, I am suggesting that the brain isn't the source of thought at all. Someone who has been indoctrinated into the mechanistic

13

paradigm and who believes we are essentially biochemical machines may find this proposition unacceptable. However it is important to continually challenge and question our long-held assumptions and realise that they are just that - assumptions, and not truths. I will elaborate on this point in the section *Challenging the Mechanistic World View.*

The functions of the brain are enormously over-estimated in traditional biology, in being considered to be the source of thought, the organ of perception, the root of creativity, the site of memory and the controller of many bodily processes. It is *possible* that the last one is true but I have serious doubts about the others. Various suggestions about what the functions of the brain are, include:

1)   The source of all human qualities - thought, consciousness, creativity, love, hate, etc.
2)   The transmitter and receiver of nerve information - both sensory and motor functions.
3)   An energy converter sending information from the external world to the essence of our being.
4)   A receiver like a television set which is tuning in to consciousness.

The most widely held belief is the first of these options, I personally believe this to be the furthest off the mark - thoughts and feelings do not arise in the brain. The source of thought that we call the mind is not *in* the brain just as the pictures are not in a television set. Someone would be considered very odd if they were to dismantle a T.V. in search of the people inside the screen! In a way, this is similar to what neuroscientists do when they analyse the brain in order to discover the exact location of the source of thought, creativity, memory, and so on. It is a strange result of scientific conditioning that those neuroscientists with these mechanistic ideas would see those of us who believe in spirit as odd. I see the brain as just an organ in the head. Of course, it is a very important organ but it's primary functions are

14

to control the bodily processes and to convert energy received from the senses into a form which can be perceived by our essence.

It is possible that the brain might be a receiver - a necessary piece of apparatus required to tune into the thoughts which YOU then observe - but the brain itself doesn't think. You may argue: "But I can feel that my thoughts are in my head". If you say this, it is probably due to a life-time of being told that you think from your brain, and the conditioning is so strong that you may now say that you can "feel" that the thoughts are in your head, but if you consider that before the days of dissection when it wasn't known what a complicated organ the brain is, people were conditioned to believe that we think from our heart and at that time they "felt" that their thoughts were located in their hearts.

Most biologists would say that when you look around you, the light forms an image on your retina at the back of your eye, but it is not the eye that sees, it is the brain that sees after the information is received from the optic nerve and processed by the brain. I would take this one step further and say that it is not the brain that "sees" but the consciousness (or soul or essence) that perceives the image after the information is received from the brain. I feel fairly sure in my own mind (but not in my brain!) that images are not formed within our brains.

Before leaving this section I want to consider one more interesting point. When we talk about states of consciousness which are not on our normal level of awareness we may use the words *higher* or *deeper* to refer to that part of us which is pure consciousness, pure energy, pure love, great wisdom, etc. Why is it that we sometimes use the word "higher" (going up), and at other times use the word "deeper" (going down), to describe altered states of consciousness? When we try to connect to this part of us are we going *up higher* or *down deeper* to reach this state? Is the *higher* self to be found *deep* within ourselves?

15

There are various ways of expressing ourselves in the English language which imply a change of level: We say that we *fall* in love; we may say that we need to *transcend* our basic instincts of aggression and get to a *higher* state of being; the word *sub*conscious implies downwards; we relax *deeply;* ecstatic feelings are described as *high,* and when we feel really good we can be on cloud nine or in seventh heaven. Hypnotists may tell their subjects that they are sinking deeper and feeling heavy or they may suggest that they are floating. Both terms, higher and deeper, imply that we are trying to connect to something on a different level. I think the different terms have entered our vocabulary due to a general western perception of God being outside of us *up there* but the source of our own spirituality being *deep inside* at the core of our being. If this is the case then the expression *fallen* in love, as opposed to *risen* in love is probably appropriate due to the fact that we are making a connection with something that is generally considered to be deep within us rather than something outside of us. It is worth adding that although each word *seems to be* conveying a slightly different meaning, the reality that the words are trying to convey is beyond words, so it is essential, in this context, to read between the lines. The "hidden" message that most religions, both east and west, seem to be conveying is that deep, deep down *at the core of my being* (inside) is universal consciousness, and that this consciousness *that we are* is everywhere around us (outside). Consciousness is both inside and outside at the same time - this is one of the paradoxes of the universe. Could it be that consciousness, soul and God are one and the same thing? Let us now consider this important question.

> ....*to remember who you are......*
> *is your sole purpose.*
> *That is to say, your soul purpose.*
> *NEALE DONALD WALSCH*

GOD AND MAN

If you have done any study of man and his relationship to the universe, you may have come across a plethora of terms to describe human and cosmic consciousness, a few examples are: Mind, awareness, thought, soul, spirit, consciousness, essence, the self, the higher self, the ego, the I, the superego, the emotional body, the mental body, the conscious mind, the unconscious mind, the preconscious mind, the subconscious mind, the universal mind, the infinite mind, God, cosmic consciousness, higher consciousness, the heavenly father, mother nature, the holy ghost, the holy spirit, eternal spirit, great spirit, the absolute, transcendence, the first cause, the infinite-eternal, the divinity, the totality, life, life-force, prana, chi, vital energy, cosmic electricity, primordial energy, universal energy, etc.

What I wonder is: "How many different concepts are there listed here?" Are they just lots of words for the same thing? Keeping in mind that all classifications are simply constructs to help us think and communicate, I want to try and classify the above words into 4 categories:
1) The mind.
2) The Observer of experience.
3) The Western God - A being looking down at us from above.
4) The Eastern God - A principle that controls everything from within. An energy that permeates the universe.

Please do not judge the category labels, since in each category I could add "for want of a better word".

After dividing them up into the four separate categories my aim is to show that they are all different facets of the same reality. Our mind fragments, divides, classifies and compartmentalises but all the division that we see around us is not a property of the universe itself, it is an illusion created by the human intellect.

17

Table 1 below shows all the above terms classified into 4 separate categories. I have highlighted the terms that I particularly like to use.

MIND	THE OBSERVER OF EXPERIENCE
Source of thought	**Essence**
Ego	**Consciousness**
Conscious mind	Awareness
Rational mind	Self
Imagination	Soul
Intellect	Spirit
	The I
	The self
	The higher self
	The deeper self
WESTERN GOD	EASTERN GOD
God	**Universal energy**
Universal mind	**Universal Consciousness**
Infinite mind	**Mother nature**
Cosmic consciousness	Great Spirit
Higher consciousness	Creative intelligence
The heavenly father	The absolute
Higher power	Eternal spirit
The holy ghost	Cosmic electricity
Jehovah	Primordial energy
Eternal spirit	Transcendence
The divinity	Life-force
The first cause	The infinite-eternal
	The totality
	Prana Chi
	Vital energy
	Creative energy

Table 1 - terms for "consciousness".

You may disagree with where I put some of these entries - this disagreement is natural and almost inevitable since we all have different conditioning and most of these words are either very vaguely defined or have no definition at all. I don't intend to justify why I included the words in the categories that I have, since the purpose of this section and the next is to show that all these words are reflecting different aspects of one reality, since the essence of our being - the consciousness which is the observer of all experience, is an intelligence that permeates the entire universe - a universal consciousness.

The western God is seen by many as a personal figure who looks down on everything controlling from outside. Many Christians see "him" as a kind of fatherly figure who possesses human-like qualities and is capable of anger, love, judgement, and so on. However, many non-christians say that this "fatherly God" is a construct of man's hopeful mind - a kind of psychological teddy bear which man has created simply for comfort.

> *Man made God in his own image.*
> *NOLAN JOHN*

The eastern view of God is very different to the western view - it is more of a living principle within all things. Eastern mystics are more likely to say "she" since they see this energy as a feminine principle which we in the west might call "mother nature".

Of all the "labels" for God in table 1, the words which I favour are those in bold print - Universal energy, Universal Consciousness and Mother nature. I also like the genderless term which the American Indians use - Great Spirit. Superficially we can say that the concept of the western God is a very different concept altogether compared with the view in the east. However, as I will explain in the next section, on a much deeper level it is possible to marry the eastern and western concepts of God.

The universe is alive, and this life which permeates all things is God - in fact the words "God" and "life" can often be used synonymously and interchangeably.

If you are agnostic or atheist, and you read a religious text that continually uses the word God, rather than think it is silly and just switch off, you can simply replace the word God by another that you prefer - I sometimes replace it with "the universe" and sometimes with "life". For example, consider a religious text that says:

> Believe that God is providing you with everything that you need. Trust in God and develop the feeling that He is on your side. Connect with God through prayer and believe that He is working for you, not against you.

If you are agnostic and you read this, you can interpret it as:

> Believe that *the universe* is providing you with everything that you need. Trust in *life* and develop the feeling that it is on your side. Connect with *the universe* through prayer (and meditation) and believe that it is working for you, not against you.

If you reinterpret religious texts in this way you may find that they hold more meaning for you, especially if you are agnostic. Conversely, if you are religious and have the more traditional view of God, you can do the reverse of this when you read a more modern spiritual text that talks about "the universe" in a way in which you are unfamiliar with.

> *The creative intelligence and energy of the universe is the fundamental source of everything. Once we connect with this and surrender to it, everything is ours.*
> SHAKTI GAWAIN

20

The main point that I am conveying here is that instead of switching off and closing your mind when you read or hear something which is expressed in a different language to what you are accustomed to, endeavour to extract the essence of the message by abstaining from judging the way that it is expressed.

I would now like to explain that all the terms in table 1 are used to communicate different aspects of the same underlying reality. For the sake of illustration I would like to compare consciousness with water (or more strictly H_2O), study the table below and then I will explain:

SOLID H_2O	GASEOUS H_2O
Ice	Steam
Icicles	Water vapour
Glacier	Fog
Snow	Cloud
	Mist
MOVING WATER	**EXPANSES OF WATER**
Fountain	Ocean
Waterfall	Sea
Rain	Lake
Flood	River
Stream	Pond
Torrent	Puddle
Rapids	Drop
Current	Bath
Splash	
Spray	
Drip	

Table 2 - terms for "water".

All the words in this table represent the same stuff which we generally call "water", but man has created all these words to facilitate communication about the state of the water or its location. In a similar way all the words in table 1 represent the same "stuff" which I like to give the general term *consciousness*. All these different words are used simply for humans to communicate different aspects of consciousness.

> *You are both a finite earthly being,*
> *and an infinite soul of great spiritual dimension.*
> *You are the drop of water and the wave.*
> *You direct yourself and you are directed.*
> CAROL ADRIENNE

Imagine transferring some pond water into the ocean - would you now say that this water is still pond water although it is now in the ocean, or is it now ocean water? If we are naming it according to its location, then once it is in the ocean we will have to call it "ocean water". Imagine now that the "pond water" has an ego and is attached to the label of "pond water" and sees this as its identity. It would not like to see itself as ceasing to exist when it changes location. But it is not ceasing to exist, only the label is ceasing to be applicable to itself. This is an extremely useful analogy to our own consciousness and identity as a separate, independent person. The "pond water" has ceased to exist because its no longer pond water, but it still lives on in another form.

Even when the water evaporates and becomes water vapour it still has not ceased to be - but its label has. Similarly when I die the label that I think of as "me" will cease to be but at the same time *I* will continue in another form. I will discuss this more in the section *life and death*.

I do like the term *creative intelligence* but the word which I tend to use most in place of God is the term *universal consciousness*, I will now discuss this in more detail.

UNIVERSAL CONSCIOUSNESS

I love the God that is my God - A life-giving source of energy, the light, the embryonic purity of each new day. This is what thrives within us and outside us and despite us. It is the eternal flame ignited by a panorama of love.
ANDREA PHOTIOU

The traditional view of a personal God who is referred to as "he" is rapidly disappearing in our society and is being replaced by a more spiritual view of God which is more akin to the definition above. Everyday, people are moving over to the view of God not as an external spirit looking down at us from outside, but a principle within all things - an energy working on everything from within. This view sees the laws of nature as being governed by a feminine principal - "mother nature" - that resides within all things, as opposed to a masculine principle - "the heavenly father" - looking down and ruling things from outside.

There is a divine purpose behind everything, and therefore a divine presence within everything.
NEIL DONALD WALSH

The eastern yogis say that when you are connected to universal consciousness you are in possession of all knowledge. Some believe that it is this universal consciousness - the font of all knowledge and wisdom - that we connect with in moments of inspiration. Others say that this font of knowledge is at the core of our soul and, at the same time, it is universal consciousness.

My own view of God is that it is an energy which permeates the entire universe - an energy which gives life to every atom and molecule in existence. Although this view is closer to the Eastern concept of "God", to some extent I also accept an aspect of the western view in that this energy is a conscious energy - a creative intelligence through which the manifest universe comes into being.

The physical world is just a mirror of a deeper intelligence. Intelligence is the invisible organiser of all matter and energy.
DR. DEEPAK CHOPRA

Since the essence of what we are is consciousness, we - who see ourselves as individuals - are a part of the universal, cosmic consciousness like droplets of ocean water immersed in the ocean. We think we are individuals but in reality we are all interconnected and our separateness is merely an illusion.

WE ARE ALL ONE

You are all the fruits of one tree and the leaves of one branch.
BAHA'I FAITH.
GLEAMINGS 132

The eastern way of looking at life is now rapidly gaining popularity in the west - this says that the universe itself is alive, everything is interconnected and there is a consciousness that runs through everything. We humans, who see ourselves as separate, individual entities are actually a part of this consciousness, but we are also all of it at the same time - this is one of the paradoxes of existence.

The most important characteristic of the Eastern world view
- one could almost say the essence of it -
is the awareness of the unity and mutual
interrelation of all things and events.
FRITJOF CAPRA

Our ego gives us the illusion that we are all separate, independent, individuals but in truth we are all interconnected - both in matter and energy. Things may seem separate but this is an error of the senses. Our bodies, which are formed by this consciousness - and not vice versa - are continually exchanging matter with our environment, so, in a way, we could consider our environment to be our extended bodies.

That which fills the universe I regard as my body,
and that which directs the universe I see as my own nature.
CHANG-TZU

Although our mentality tends to separate and categorise things which results in a fragmented view of the universe, this view is actually a delusion created by our limited perception and is not actually how the universe itself really is. The universe, as described by all the greatest teachers throughout history, can be best described as one mass of material immersed in one energy field of which we, who see ourselves as individuals, are just a part of. Even this statement is very limited, but inherently so since it is trying to describe the indescribable. In an *attempt* to go beyond words I could say that the mass *is* the energy field, and we are not really just a part of it all but we are it all. **You are not just a part of the universe, you are the universe.** Please note that you are not meant to "comprehend" this statement because the intellect is designed to divide and compartmentalise; we see ourselves as separate entities because that is how our intellect is designed to perceive.

If we could transcend the intellect and directly see things as they really are, (as in a spiritual or so-called "religious" experience), we would perceive the unity and mutual interrelation of all things and events.

> *You are not enclosed within your bodies,*
> *nor confined to houses or fields.*
> *That which is you dwells above the mountain*
> *and roves with the wind.*
> KAHLIL GIBRAN

One way of expressing the profundity of this concept is to say that our higher self or essence which is the conscious observer of all our experience is the same consciousness that permeates every atom and molecule in the universe. The manifest universe is immersed in this ocean of consciousness, in fact it only becomes manifest because of it.

> *There is but one mind,*
> *every man is an inlet to that one mind....*
> RALPH WALDO EMERSON

Each of us are instruments through which shines the light of consciousness. A good analogy is that of many torches which are supplied by the same power source - each shines their own light even though the power source is the same.

> *I am you;*
> *The light of consciousness is one,*
> *but it is shone through different instruments*
> *which give the illusion of separateness.*
> DR. KATHERINE WATSON

The analogy between us as instruments which shine the light of consciousness and torches would be even more complete if we could say that the power source not only lights them up but also creates the torches themselves, in other words, our bodies are a manifestation of the light of consciousness.

The great physicist Albert Einstein was aware of our connection with the universe as the following quotation shows. Referring to the human being he stated:

> *He experiences himself, his thoughts and feelings*
> *as something separated from the rest - a kind*
> *of optical delusion of consciousness.*
> ALBERT EINSTEIN

All of the wisest human beings in history have tried to express the realisation of our interconnectedness as the ultimate state we can achieve. This cannot be just an intellectual realisation but must be an experiential realisation, in the east this state of consciousness is referred to as Samadhi, and in the west it is known as enlightenment.

The realisation that there is no separateness makes us see all of life in a new light. The idea of unity relates not only to us in relation to the universe, but also to us as individuals who are torn apart by internal conflict.

A useful model for the human being, consistent with that given by the eastern yogis, is that we consist of a physical body, a mental body (the mind) and an emotional body (the spirit). Our body, mind and emotions may often pull in different directions causing inner turmoil within us. If we are feeling miserable, we are feeling separate. The yogi says that inner harmony comes from uniting the three bodies - the physical body, the mental body and the emotional body. In fact, the word yoga means to "join together" or "sum up". When we can achieve this inner harmony we will be connected with the essence of our being which is the totality of life.

*You can never be lonely if you experience
your aloneness as all-oneness.*

If you ever feel disconnected or lonely it means you are not fully conscious. To be "fully conscious" is synonymous with "to be in a blissful state of love" which is also synonymous with "to be at one with the universe". Tennyson described experiencing this feeling of being at one with everything in moments of peace and all-oneness, in the following quotation:

*...Individuality itself seemed to dissolve and fade away into
boundless being, and this is not a confused state but
the clearest of the clear, the surest of the sure,
utterly beyond words, where death was
almost a laughable impossibility....*
TENNYSON

When Jesus called himself "the son of God" he was acknowledging his connection with the universal spirit, higher consciousness, light of consciousness, energy of the universe, divine love, the infinite mind, mother nature, eternal spirit, the absolute, the transcendence, life, the infinite-eternal, the totality, the higher power, the ultimate reality, cosmic intelligence, the light, or whatever you like to call it. He managed to get rid of the barriers that separate most of us from our inner wisdom - that wisdom which is universal consciousness.

Buddha had a similar realisation as Jesus - he realised his oneness with the universe by getting rid of all internal barriers set up by our attachment to material things and our categorising mentalities that tend to label everything and hence create the illusion of separateness.

Your own Self
lives in the heart of all.
THE UPANISHAD

We will feel the optimum level of health, happiness and inner peace, when, as well as being in harmony with ourselves, we are also interacting harmoniously with the universe. As we progress along the spiritual path and become connected to our spiritual essence more of the time, we become more sensitive to the needs of others - not only people but animals and plants also. In fact we become aware that the earth itself is a living organism as explained by the Gaia theory.

Man's heart away from Nature becomes hard.
Lack of respect for growing, living things
soon leads to lack of respect for humans.
LAKOTA (AMERICAN INDIAN) PROVERB

As we realise the illusion of our separateness with all of life, exploitation is replaced by conservation, and ecological and planetary issues become of much greater importance.

We are but one strand in the web of life -
every time we abuse the environment,
we are abusing ourselves.

It is when we are *fully conscious* that confusion turns into understanding, resentment turns into compassion, vengeance turns into forgiveness, denial turns into acceptance, and sorrow turns into peaceful contentment. **Living with full awareness has a transforming effect.** This level of expanded consciousness comes when we are in a state of love and connectedness with all

29

of life. In this state of consciousness we realise that life truly does have meaning, and that the blind way that we often conduct our lives comes from the illusion of seeing ourselves as separate entities, disconnected from the rest of the universe.

But how do we become "fully conscious"? The answer lies in living life fully in each moment, and to develop a love and a trust for life and appreciate every experience that the universe offers us for our development.

> *Love is the guiding force which enables us*
> *to see the unity in all things.*

It is clear that what Jesus meant when he said "the kingdom of heaven is within you", is that the path to true happiness, inner peace, love, compassion and great wisdom are not somewhere to be found outside of us - and will not come by attachment to doctrine - but are within each of us. If we can get in touch with the deepest, spiritual part of our being then we will no longer need to search the world for what we are looking for - everything that we could wish for is within us.

> *The kingdom of heaven is within you*
> *and whoever knows himself shall find it.*
> *And, having found it, you shall know yourselves*
> *that you are in God and God is in you.*
> *And you are the kingdom of God.*
> *JESUS CHRIST*

To summarise, when we are totally in harmony with ourselves and with the universe and cease to function from the ego, we realise that our individuality is just an error of the senses and we are just as much a part of the universe as the land and the sky.

So be one with this land
and be one with the sky
and don't be afraid to be you.
ANDREA PHOTIOU

The individual, the family, the community, the nation, and the whole of humanity needs to give way to fragmentation and find unity.

Under the light of consciousness
there is no East and West, only unity.
DR. KATHERINE WATSON

NATIONAL BORDERS
ARE A HUMAN CONSTRUCT

Can there be any human activity more insane than
to kill another human being because he happened to be born
the other side of the border?

In its present state the human race has many failings created primarily by the darkness which is a result of being disconnected from our essence. I believe that the reason that this situation has arisen is because we are, as a race, systematically kept from the true knowledge which would allow us to realise our true potential. I am referring to that knowledge which was possessed by the American Indians, the Aborigines, the Tibetan monks, and many Shamans throughout history. All these races and cultures have been systematically murdered, tortured, imprisoned, and the knowledge which they had access to either destroyed or suppressed by those who run this planet.

Being separated from "source" (our true essence or universal consciousness) has the result that we are much easier to manipulate, this is very convenient for the planetary rulers. We have been divided and conquered and the loving spirit of humanity quashed to the extent that people can be made to kill each other for absolutely ridiculous reasons.

> *Prejudice is one of the world's greatest labour saving devices;*
> *it enables you to form an opinion without*
> *having to dig up the facts.*
> *LAURENCE PETER*

Once we can come to accept that we are all one, we will realise that whenever we insult, abuse or exploit another person or our environment we are committing an offence against ourselves.

> *See all living beings on this planet as one;*
> *fragmentation and division are the main problems*
> *in our outlook towards ourselves, our family*
> *and our planetary society.*

The native American Indians new this, they were a beautiful race living in harmony with the land and the whole of nature. I believe they knew the secrets related to our true potential, had absolutely no fear of death and saw everything as sacred.

> *The rainstorm and the river are my brothers;*
> *The Heron and the Dolphin are my friends;*
> *And we are all connected to each other,*
> *in a circle, in a hoop, that never ends.*
> *POCAHONTAS*

The genocide of the native Americans is one of the saddest events in human history. Chief Seattle, a wise and gentle man had this to say of the white man's blindness:

.....to harm the Earth is to reap contempt on its Creator. When the last Redman has vanished from the Earth, and the memory is only the shadow of a cloud moving across the prairie, these shores and forests will still hold the spirits of my people, for they love the Earth as the newborn loves its mother's heartbeat.

If we sell you our land, love it as we have cared for it. Hold it in your mind, the memory of the land as it is when you take it. And with all your strength, with all your might, and with all your heart, preserve it for your children and love it as God loves us all. One thing we know, our God is the same God. This Earth is precious to Him......

We cannot buy or sell the sky, or the warmth of the land. We do not own the freshness of the air, or the sparkle of the water. Every part of the Earth is sacred. Every shining pine needle. Every sandy shore. Every mist in the dark woods.......

But to the white man one portion of land is the same as the next. The Earth is an enemy which is there to be conquered. He kidnaps the Earth for his children. He does not care. His appetite will devour the Earth and leave behind only a desert.

There is no quiet place in the cities. No place to hear the waves of the spring or the rustle of insect's wings. The clatter only seems to insult the ears. The Indian prefers the soft sound of the wind darting over the *face of the pond, and the smell of the wind itself cleansed by the midday rain or scented with pine.*

The air is precious to the Redman, for all things share the same breath - the beasts, the trees, the man..... All things are connected. Whatever befalls the Earth, befalls the sons of the Earth.

How sad that they weren't listened to with the love and respect they deserved. But there spirit is strong and lives on in many ways.

It is tragic how many millions have died simply due to the attachment to a certain belief system or even worse because of the colour of their skin or the country where they were born. Can anything be more ridiculous than to judge a person on the basis of their skin colour or the place that they happened to be born. I have always found it incredibly sad that anyone can possibly do this. To illustrate how ridiculous this is, imagine living in a society where everyone is judged by whether their hair is straight or curly, or even worse, where straight haired people kill curly haired people for no other reason than because their hair is curly. Does this sound ridiculous? Well I find all earthly prejudice - racial, social, political, religious, or whatever, is as *equally* ridiculous as this.

> *Falsely seeing the world as one of separate, fragmented entities is what causes antagonism, greed, and inevitably suffering.*
> *THE BUDDHA*

Imagine for a moment that countries were not given names and that the planet earth was simply one big country. This image makes the futility of war even clearer since it shows that one group of men may be killing another group simply because they happened to be born on a different area of land.

If only we could all transcend the attachment to the label of "my country" and replace it with a devotion for not only our country but for the whole of humanity, then the world would become one and earthly conflict would cease.

I find not only racism to be an extremely sad state of mind but also religious bigotry, nationalism, and any other "divided" mentality that gives rise to these states of mind. Even patriotism can be a very negative quality because it is usually based on a feeling of superiority to the place where one lives as opposed to a mutual respect of all countries, races and cultures. The justification of "fighting for *my* country" can be seen in a clearer light when you consider that your soul could just as easily have been born and raised in "their" country and you would then be your own enemy! All this is obviously nonsense and illustrates how the human race has been indoctrinated and manipulated into a disharmonious situation. For many reasons I believe that this situation has arisen because it is of great benefit to those who rule the planet. For more information about this topic read any of David Icke's inspiring books particularly *I am me, I am free,* published by Bridge of love.

It is not for him to pride himself for loving his own country, but rather for him to love the whole world.
The earth is but one country, and mankind its citizens.
BAHA'I FAITH, GLEANINGS 117

I would like to end this section with a few sentences extracted from the end of my book *You Really are Responsible* in the section *Towards a peaceful world:*

Imagine the whole planet living in unity - then there could
be no wars - you may say I'm a dreamer, but I'm not the only
one!

> *Imagine there's no countries, it isn't hard to do.*
> *Nothing to kill or die for, and no religion too.*
> *Imagine all the people living life in peace......*
> *JOHN LENNON*

As the world evolves, and awareness increases, barriers will
slowly break down and the planet will become more united.
As this happens the suffering caused by the whole host of
racial and social prejudices will diminish within the world -
maybe this will come true sooner than we expect.

> *I have a dream.......*
> *.......that children will be judged on the basis of*
> *the content of their character, not the colour of their skin.*
> *.......I have a dream,*
> *that the brotherhood of man will become a reality in this day.*
> *And with this faith I will go out and carve a tunnel*
> *of hope through the mountain of despair.*
> *With this faith I will go out with you*
> *and transform dark yesterdays into bright tomorrows.*
> *With this faith we will be able to*
> *achieve this new day when all of God's children -*
> *black men and white men,*
> *Jews and Gentiles, Protestants and Catholics,*
> *will be able to join hands and sing with*
> *the Negro in a spiritual abode:*
> *"free at last, free at last, thank God we're free at last".*
> *MARTIN LUTHER KING*
> *(28/8/63)*

IS THE HUMAN SOUL
GOOD OR BAD?

I have, for many years, asked myself the very important question: "Is humanity essentially good or bad?" The two statements below encompass the two possible viewpoints regarding human nature: Which one do you hold to?

1) Human nature is inconsiderate, nasty and selfish. It is not our nature to be good, kind and considerate to others but we learn these qualities so that we are able to live in peace, and if we are good it is only for selfish reasons so that we can make ourselves feel better.
OR

2) We are, in essence, wonderful, loving beings. Human nature is good, but we learn to be selfish and hard because we live in a cruel competitive world and there are many factors which block us from our loving essence.

Which view is correct, are we born good or bad? The idea of the higher self and the ego can combine these two points of view and show that they are both true in some respects.

The ego functions from instinct, just trying to satisfy selfish wants, needs and desires. It is far from spiritual, it is the part of us that gives rise to negativity, greed, jealousy, anger, resentment, condemnation, hate, judgement, and so on. This part of the human being is sometimes referred to as the basic self.

If by human nature we mean "the essence of what we are", and this is what I believe is the case, then we are, by nature, good and so the answer to the above question is that the human soul is definitely good. We only appear bad when blocks arise which separate us from our essential nature, and then the ego starts to rule our behaviour.

*They are forever free who renounce all selfish desires
and break away from the ego-cage of "I", "me" and "mine"
to be united with the lord.*
THE BAHA'I FAITH

If we could remove the barriers that usually exist between our ego-mind and our spiritual essence, which is the source of love and wisdom, then all evil, selfish thoughts would disappear - we could then say that we are functioning from the higher self. Our higher self is the part of us that functions from the spiritual values such as appreciation of beauty, quest for truth, acceptance, compassion, joy, creativity, intuition, trust, honesty, loyalty, integrity, giving, caring, openness, inspiration, and, of course, love.

If you allow your ego, or basic self, to govern your behaviour, you will give out "negative vibes" and according to the law of cause and effect, you will receive what you give out. In other words, if you are living from the ego you won't receive much positive energy in your interactions. Conversely, if your higher self governs the way that you live, then you will not want to harm any living creature, life will be exciting, you will throw out positive energy, and you will therefore receive more joy, peace, harmony, inspiration and love.

A man's wisdom increases with his ability to function from his higher self. If you can learn to connect to this part of yourself then you will become more open, loving, compassionate and wise.

But what creates the blocks in the first place so that the ego takes charge? How can we release these blocks and make contact with the beautiful, wise, loving essence that we are? This question is well worth considering because if we can remove these blocks our life will improve beyond measure. The path to oneness is not easy - it requires a number of lifestyle adjustments which I will explain in the section *Practical Steps To Enlightenment.*

LIFE AND DEATH

You don't get to choose how you're going to die, or when.
You can only decide how you are going to live. Now.
JOAN BAEZ.

Probably the two most difficult things that we have to accept in life are the death of someone we love, and the fact that we are going to die. In our society death tends to be a somewhat taboo subject with many people preferring not to talk or even think about. This may often be due to the fact that we have trouble coming to terms with our own mortality, but it may also be due to the fact that we don't want to look at our fears and attachments related to losing the ones we love.

On no subject are our ideas more
warped and pitiable than on death.
JOHN MUIR

There are various ways that difficult or challenging experiences can be dealt with. In the case of the death of a loved one we can develop a positive view of death so that it is not so painful, or we can suppress and deny the pain by forming around ourselves an "emotional safety barrier". The latter is not an option that I recommend as I shall now explain.

I used to have a friend who told me that he could never get emotionally hurt. I found this difficult to believe and asked him how he was able to achieve such an amazing feat. He told me that his first experiences with a special girl friend who he loved and lost upset him enormously and therefore he decided that from that time onwards he was going to be "thick-skinned" and not allow himself to be hurt again, he decided to develop the attitude that things would not bother him anymore. He built a kind of emotional and psychological wall around himself which would stop him from getting hurt. An interesting side-effect to this was that he actually became a less sensitive person - less emotional in every way - so as well as stopping bad experiences from effecting him, this "emotional safety barrier" that he created, also stopped him from being able to fully experience good feelings.

A man's armour can block his amour.
NOLAN JOHN

I realised that many people do this to some extent, either consciously or unconsciously. They go through life with an emotional safety barrier around them which, although it stops them from being too vulnerable, it also stops them from feeling love, affection, joy, happiness, and other wonderful feelings that come when we allow ourselves to be open and sensitive.

The worst sin towards our fellow creatures is not to hate them, but to be indifferent to them; that's the essence of inhumanity.
GEORGE BERNARD SHAW.

It is interesting that most people want to be sensitive but they don't want to be vulnerable. In truth these are two different words for the same human quality based on the ability to feel. Vulnerability simply implies that what you are sensitive to may cause you pain. Most of the time the emotional pain is caused by our attachments. We want things to be a certain way and if they are not how we want them to be then we suffer.

In resisting pain and suffering we may consciously or unconsciously erect barriers to make us tougher, but these barriers also make us less "alive" in the full sense of the word.

To be indifferent is "the essence of inhumanity" because we live to feel - whether it be joy, sadness, love, hate, affection, anger or any other emotion - to feel something is better, or at least more human, than to feel nothing at all.

....all feelings are part of the wonderful, ever-changing sensation of being alive.
SHAKTI GAWAIN

All the feelings that most of us experience as "normal" human beings are stepping stones on the way to a constant state of love, joy and bliss. To get to this state we must treat all negative feelings as messengers that can teach us something and then make adjustments in our consciousness so we are not affected in exactly the same way after.

When we shut ourselves off from potential feelings because of the fear of pain, we are also separating ourselves from the true pleasure of living. We live to connect - both with nature and with people, so it is important to slowly try and break down the walls that we have built up around ourselves and learn to connect and to love, even though due to our increased sensitivity we could get hurt more easily. If we are able to achieve this peaceful acceptance of our own vulnerability, we will appreciate more the immense beauty that surrounds us and begin to see how valuable life really is.

When we fully open our feelings to life,
our increased sensitivity enables us to truly
experience the joy of being alive.

41

In the case of the death of a loved one, the difficulty is not only due to missing someone you love but also in coming to terms with an irreversible loss. If someone you love dies, your suffering will only stop when you can come to terms with the fact that they have gone, they are not coming back, that is the hand that life dealt and you must come to terms with it, accept it, and get on with your own life. You can, however, keep in mind that you may very probably see them again one day!

Each player must accept the cards life deals him or her:
But once they are in hand, he or she alone must decide
how to play the cards in order to win the game.
VOLTAIRE

We need to learn to go with the flow and accept life as it is - this includes allowing the possibility of the pain of loss and tragedy to arise, while realising that if it does we will come through the loss and eventually develop a peaceful acceptance.

If you have recently become bereaved and are having trouble coming to terms with your new situation, you can take a lot of comfort in knowing that the difficult time that you are now passing through is helping you to develop more than you could have previously imagined.

Nothing ever happens to any man that
he is not formed by nature to bear.
MARCUS AURELIUS ANTONINUS

Once we are able to face, one of the hardest experiences that anyone can face - losing a loved one - and move passed the denial and resistance, then the acceptance, once it comes, will provide an inner peace which will strengthen us in such a way that we will then find ourselves prepared to handle any trials that life offers us.

The pain does not have to be deep and enduring
if you have absorbed the reality of life as an eternal flow
in which there is no loss or gain, only transformation.
DR DEEPAK CHOPRA

We are incredibly adaptable creatures. We have the inner capabilities to handle almost any situation that we find ourselves in. If we feel that we can't cope when we initially confront new experiences, this is only a temporary feeling and within a short time we learn to adapt and do what is required to handle the situation. When we are ready to let go of the grief then it will simply evaporate.

Time is a physician that heals every grief.
DIPHILIUS

Actually I believe that it is not time that does the healing, but the awareness that comes in time that teaches us how to let go of the attachments that cause the pain.

Death is such a natural thing - it is simply part of the process of renewal. If death didn't exist then neither would life - they go hand in hand together. They are inseparable partners like the two poles of a magnet - one cannot exist without the other. Every death makes way for new life.

We live in a beautifully balanced system
in which death is a part of everything that lives.
The pain of our personal loss is ours;
Within the greater whole, nothing is lost.
KAREN CASEY / MARTHA VANCEBURG

The more people that we love the greater is our risk of grief. But love is what we live for, and to prevent love from entering our lives due to fear of losing that love is the saddest fear of all.

> *It is better to have loved and lost,*
> *than never to have loved at all.*
> FRANCIS BACON

Just as life and death are two inseparable properties of nature, so are love and grief, these go hand in hand - the greater the love, the greater is usually the grief when that love is lost.

> *The price we pay for living is dying.*
> *The price we pay for loving is grief.*
> ANDREA PHOTIOU

For many, the fear is not that of losing a loved one but of having to face their own death. A strong fear of death can force you into a life of torment where nothing has any meaning.

> *The fear of death is more to be*
> *dreaded than death itself.*
> PUBLILIUS SYRUS

If someone lives with a fear of death, both their own and their loved ones, then their fear can diminish the quality of life to such an extent that they can't be happy and enjoy life anyway. What a sad situation we would be in if the reason we can't truly live is because we don't want to die!

> *Unless you fully accept the inevitability of death,*
> *it's hard to enjoy this interval called life.*
> JOHN-ROGER/PETER MCWILLIAMS

44

Mankind suffers so much because of the difficulty he has in coming to terms with the fact that nothing is permanent. Many people say that the belief in "life after death" is only a comforting belief which man creates because he doesn't like to imagine himself ceasing to be. However, this is only an issue when we strongly attach to our label as an individual person. As I explained in the section *God and Man* although in one respect it is true to say that nothing is permanent, in another way it is also true that nothing is impermanent either - only the form changes, or more to the point - our label of the form.

> *All things are impermanent;*
> *but all things are eternal also.*

If your worry is related to your own mortality, you can possibly take heart in discoveries that have been made in recent years into the *near death experience.* Considerable evidence has been found to suggest that our awareness continues after the death of the physical body.

> *If life is the sentence*
> *then death is the release.*
> NOLAN JOHN

Many people who have been declared dead on the operating table and then resuscitated have recounted experiences of leaving their physical bodies and watching the resuscitation attempt from a vantage point above their physical bodies. They talk of floating upwards and seeing their body lying below them, they then go through a dark tunnel and encounter a bright light which radiates love and helps to guide them in their new experience.

Those who have experienced "dying" speak of meeting up with dead relatives and friends who have come to greet them and feel a profound sense of peace and love, so much so that they often

45

speak of feeling saddened when they discover that it's not their time yet and they have to return to their bodies to continue living their lives.

The spirit kills not, nor is it killed.
It was not born; it will never die.
Nor once having been, can it ever cease to be:
Unborn, Eternal, Ever-enduring, yet most ancient,
the Spirit dies not when the body is dead.
.......Knowing the Spirit as such, thou hast no cause to grieve.
BHAGAVAD GEETA

Nearly everyone who has had these "near death experiences" has said that afterwards their lives changed immensely for the better because life now seems, without a doubt, to have a deeper meaning.

Some say death is such a wonderful experience
that the news must be kept from us
or we'd all be killing ourselves just to get there.
JOHN-ROGER/PETER MCWILLIAMS

In his book *"life after life"* Dr Raymond Moody Jr. compiled case histories of people who have experienced "dying" and given accounts of the experiences that they went through. Below are a few extracts taken from his book:

> "I began to experience the most wonderful feelings. I couldn't feel a thing in the world except peace, comfort, ease - just quietness. I felt that all my troubles were gone, and I thought to myself, "well how quiet and peaceful, and I don't hurt at all."

46

"I remember being wheeled into the operating room and the next few hours were the critical period. During that time, I kept getting in and out of my physical body, and I could see it from above. But, while I did, I was still in a body - not a physical body, but something I can best describe as an energy pattern. If I had to put it into words, I would say that it was transparent, a spiritual as opposed to a material being."

"Since I died, all of a sudden, right after my experience, I started wondering whether I had been doing the things I had done because they were good, or because they were good for me....................it seems that the understanding I have of things now is so much better. I feel like this is because of what happened to me, because of the places I went and the things I saw in this experience."

Almost without exception, everyone who has been through the near death experience, speaks of it positively - not only in terms of it being a wonderful experience but also for the positive effect it has on their lives afterwards. They tend to become less egotistical and materialistic and more altruistic and spiritual. Most importantly they lose all fear of death and realise that life does, after all, have a purpose. Here are six quotations which convey the point that death is something which by no means should be feared.

*Nothing can happen
more beautiful than death.*
  WALT WHITMAN

It is impossible that anything so natural, so necessary,
and so universal as death, should ever have been designed
by providence as an evil to mankind.
JONATHAN SWIFT

People living deeply have no fear of death.
ANAIS NIN

There is no great tragedy involved in leaving the body.
In many ways the tragedy is being in the body.
NEALE DONALD WALSCH.

Death is not the end of life.....
it is the beginning.
NOLAN JOHN

Energy cannot be created or destroyed only transformed.
Therefore you have no need to fear death,
just see it as a transformation from
the physical to the spiritual.
THOMAS ALLEN

At the time of completing the final manuscript of this book, just before going to print, my father's body ceased to function as a vehicle to carry his spirit. This was very sad because he was a wonderful man and was loved by everyone who new him especially his five devoted sons and daughters. Within two days of his transition I received a letter from the spirit world channelled by Jan Pendragon*. Here is a section of this letter:

There is no need to be sad, for there is so much that you don't realise whilst in the body that confines your

*Jan Pendragon, along with her husband Mike Pendragon run the *Conversations with God* institute in Manchester.

spirit, and your father is now experiencing the fulfilment of his life. For while in your bodies you go through all kinds of incredible experiences whilst your soul seeks the freedom it desires. And when it is finally released there is an overwhelming sense of incredible lightness and freedom as the love that you are is experienced in its fullness. For now he sees things clearly, be glad that he is now free of the body that confines, and is so happy that you are helping so many understand what he now understands.......

We can look upon death as an exciting adventure. Make it your aim to tell yourself in your final moments of this phase of your existence "and now the really exciting journey begins!"

> *To be or not to be, that is the question........*
> *for in that sleep of death what dreams may come,*
> *when we have shuffled off this mortal coil....*
> WILLIAM SHAKESPEARE

The following beautiful poem called "Dear death" conveys the point that, not only should we not fear death but we should be grateful for it.

> *Dear death, were you not there, what to life would I compare?*
> *How could I measure time, and appreciate what is mine?*
> *But existing as you do, I compare sweet life with you,*
> *like a glow against the night, you keep life in my sight.*
> ANDREA PHOTIOU

CHALLENGING THE MECHANISTIC WORLD VIEW

I would now like to discuss an alternative to the world view that most of us who went to school were indoctrinated to believe without question. The western educational system usually mis-educates pupils to believe a doctrine as if it is fact when in truth it is based on numerous assumptions which are all open to question. I am of course referring to the scientific paradigm which is so highly respected in the west today. It is important to be aware that the current so-called scientific paradigm which is based on a world view that sees the universe as functioning like a giant machine governed by eternal laws is only one of many possible world views.

Throughout most of the history of mankind, matter has been considered as being alive, and it was generally accepted that there is a living principle within all things that govern the laws of nature. It is only relatively recently, in historical terms, that, in the west at least, matter was "declared dead" and that the laws of nature were considered to be governed by "an external spiritual being" looking down at everything from above. This change of view was brought about by the mechanistic science of Newtonian physics in the Seventeenth century.

When this change of view of the universe came about, there was a corresponding change of view of what we are - an inanimate physical body with a spiritual being residing within it. It was René Descartes in the Seventeenth century who formulated this dualistic philosophy that mind and matter are totally separate. It is he who put forward the view that we are a conscious mind residing within a body which is essentially "dead" matter.

Isaac Newton was the founder of the mechanistic world view, which formed the basis of the deterministic, classical physics

50

which became the dominant scientific world view up to the beginning of the twentieth century. (It was replaced by Einsteinian relativity and Quantum theory) This is the world-view that perpetrated into the public mentality and today most of the lay community in the western world thinks in a mechanistic Newtonian way (many lay people still function from an Aristotelian mindset).

After Newtonian physics became established, the next degenerative change that occurred within the traditional scientific world view was to drop "spirit" altogether. Human beings, and all life, was then seen as a clump of inanimate matter put together in a very complex way so as to give rise to the phenomenon of thought, consciousness, creativity, memory, and so on. In fact, every mental, emotional or spiritual phenomena was reduced to being the result of electrochemical activity in the brain and nervous system - sadly, there are still many scientists who continue to hold to this very limited, narrow viewpoint.

In fact, many scientists go further and say that animals don't think, and have no consciousness, (they usually assume that thought and consciousness are the same thing). Their belief is that animals just function on instinct, and these instincts are created by programmes stored in complex molecules of DNA within their cells. I believe that the role of DNA is enormously over-estimated in traditional biology, many scientists would say that it determines *everything* about the human being - the structure and function of the body, our behaviour, our personality, our intelligence, our awareness, and so on.

I believe that the true role of DNA is only a fraction of what is presently considered to be the case. It might be that the DNA only holds the small amount of information necessary to direct the chemical processes that occur within each cell (or maybe not even that). It is important to be aware that the *belief* that DNA

51

controls everything, is just that - *a belief* created by an assumption based on the materialistic world view.

Scientists have been trained to be "objective" as if it is a wonderful quality, this is based on another assumption that there is an independent reality *out there* which is totally independent of our thoughts, beliefs, attitudes, hopes or wishes. So any accurate description of reality within this scientific paradigm, has needed to be one which is totally independent of the observer. But now, with the development of quantum theory, this objectivity is disappearing as physicists are realising the importance of considering the observer when trying to understand the observed - acknowledging that there is an intrinsic interconnection between all things.

It is just as important to consider the role of consciousness in the process of observation, as it is to look at the object being observed.

I would go so far as to say that the doctrine of objectivity that perpetrates mainstream science is guaranteed to keep us from finding the truth since objectivity requires that we don't consider the wants, desires, needs, hopes, aspirations or dreams of the consciousness undergoing the act of observation. What a narrow, one-sided view this is. The power of consciousness is immense, in fact I believe that consciousness is co-creating all the phenomena that "it" is observing. If this is true then the dogma of objectivity is truly a ridiculous one.

The mechanistic world view has led to an incredibly limiting narrow-mindedness among those who attach to it. Those who have been indoctrinated into this belief system also attach to the biochemical model of living beings and the germ theory of disease, they will reject out of hand any model which isn't explainable in mechanistic terms such as homeopathy, spiritual healing, magnetic therapies, etc. If we use the energetic model of the human body all of these therapies are easily explainable, it is only when we dogmatically attach to the scientific paradigm that we may claim that these therapies are "inexplicable".

The most severe limitation of the mechanistic paradigm is its inability to explain what life is or how it arises. The inevitable end-point of mechanistic reasoning is that "we are simply a bundle of chemicals". The spiritual world view explains what life is, how it arises and what part we as humans play in the whole scheme of things.

Traditional science is based on materialist models which *assume* that consciousness is caused by brain processes, whereas the reverse could just as easily be true - the chemical processes that are going on in our brains, as well as every other part of our bodies, might be *a result of* our consciousness.

The traditional mechanistic world view sees our consciousness *as a product of* biochemical reactions that occur within our brain. The alternative, spiritual world view moves us towards the idea that our consciousness *determines* the biochemical reactions that occur within our brain. In other words, the biochemical reactions, and indeed all living physiological processes are a result of consciousness. The mechanistic world view sees the invisible as arising from the visible whereas an equally valid alternate view is that the visible arises from the invisible. I believe that they are inextricably linked.

The biochemistry of the body is a product of awareness.
Beliefs, thoughts, and emotions create the chemical
reactions that uphold life in every cell.
DR. DEEPAK CHOPRA

53

This spiritual world view at least moves us in the direction towards explaining a very mysterious problem of life - the differentiation of cells in a developing foetus.

The reason for the mystery is that each cell contains the same genetic information - that of the original zygote produced by the fusion of sperm and ovum, in other words, every cell is initially identical. When the zygote divides, it becomes two cells, then four, then eight, then sixteen, and so on, until it is a clump of millions of *identical* cells. Following this it forms into specialised groups of cells.

A traditional biologist indoctrinated into the mechanistic world view which assumes that bodily structure is programmed by the DNA within the nucleus of each cell has no idea why some cells decide to become a hand, others a heart, others nerve cells, and so on. The reason that this is so difficult to understand is because each cell is initially *identical* in every way, so why should they become so different? Why do the cells not remain the same as they divide? What causes them to differentiate?

The spiritual, energetic world view moves us towards an explanation of this incredible phenomenon by postulating that there exists a "field of awareness" or an intelligence within the universe that matter moulds itself to - a kind of cosmic blueprint or spiritual field that is present before the cells of a developing foetus form into an organism of the appropriate species. So, it could be the case that, upon fertilisation, an "etheric template" is formed along with the zygote which then guides the cells into position and holds the information that determines which type of cells they become. I believe that it is this energy field which guides the growth, healing and physiological processes of life throughout our time within this body.

A SILLY QUESTION:
IS THERE LIFE ELSEWHERE?

Mankind has always pondered the question "Is there life elsewhere in the universe?" It used to be thought that life is such an improbable occurrence that the chance of it randomly occurring anywhere is very close to zero. It was also believed that the conditions have to be "just right" for life to occur and that these perfect conditions occur only on earth and the chance of another planet existing with conditions similar to earth which can support life is very remote. I heard one scientist express the view that "the probability of life occurring is the same as if you were to throw thousands of bricks into the air and have them fall down to form a house!" This is an extremely limited view based on the mechanistic paradigm, which says that life may occur by some fluke of nature only if atoms get together in just the right way. This silly idea that life is an improbable event is based on the assumption that we live in a dead universe without any organising intelligence and every particle's movement is governed simply by mechanistic mathematical laws - what a simple-minded assumption!

Life is much more likely to be not a result of random events, but an intrinsic property of the universe itself. It might be the case that *every* star in the universe may have a planet orbiting around it which is capable of supporting some kind of life.

Possibly all that is required for life-forms to evolve is an energy source - or do I say this because of my own indoctrination into the scientific, mechanistic, deterministic world view which expounds doctrines as if they are truths such as the law of conservation of matter and energy, the second law of thermodynamics, the inevitable increase of entropy (or disorder), etc. The mechanistic world view would see this energy source as the sun or a star, whereas a more spiritual world view sees the source of energy as the prana or "light" which permeates every atom of the universe. Every material body in the universe is immersed in this prana, so maybe an external energy source such as a burning star isn't an essential prerequisite, after all, for life to exist. The universe may be bathed in an energy field of infinite potential - in fact there is now considerable evidence for this. Scientists call it the zero point energy.

> *The zero point energy in one cubic centimetre*
> *of space is said to equal the energy available*
> *in a million, million tons of uranium.*
> *This is virtually limitless energy.*
> GABRIEL COUSENS

Many sages and enlightened beings have taught that energy comes before form, that there is some kind of etheric template that exists before the physical form which the biological life form moulds itself to. A great scientist called Nikola Tesla said that our bodies exist as a precipitation out of an invisible, unbounded, energy of infinite potential. Gabriel Cousens calls these energy patterns *subtle organising energy fields* which he describes as templates for biological forms and structures. The more one looks into the subject of life and the universe the more evidence appears that the manifest universe arises out of the invisible. Consciousness is the ultimate "stuff" of the universe, not matter.

The view that life is a property of the universe takes us into a deeper understanding of life in the universe and leads us to what I consider is a much more interesting question than "is there life elsewhere? The question that I like to ask in place of this one is: "Is there any place in the universe where life doesn't exist?" I sincerely believe that **there is nowhere in the universe where life doesn't exist.** This viewpoint based on a living universe also suggests that life evolving on Earth isn't an improbable occurrence at all - it is an inevitable occurrence.

I am talking about life here, as "the intrinsic intelligence within all atoms which give them the ability to assemble into structures which are capable of exchanging energy with their environment". You may say that "this is not what I think of as life, I see it as the property of sentient beings like animals and plants here on earth." My answer to this is that sentient beings are the inevitable result of matter interactions in a living universe. The whole universe is alive and gives rise to sentient beings wherever and whenever it can.

I believe that life is literally everywhere - it is the essential property of the universe itself. It is possible that life-forms like bacteria may be present around *every star* in the universe. A few years ago I might have thought that this view is going a little too far but a type of bacteria has been discovered in volcanic larva which can survive at extremely high temperatures and therefore I now consider the possibility that there could be life-forms even *within* a star. However, if we assume that the evolution of more developed sentient beings require certain conditions which I believe may be present in, or around, at least 1 in 100 stars then it may still be that the universe is teeming with sentient life forms.

If this estimate is correct there are *sentient beings* on planetary systems revolving around at least 1000 000 000 stars in every galaxy in the universe. Since the universe is considered to contain 100, 000, 000, 000 galaxies, this means that there may be 10^{20} (one followed by 20 zeros, or one hundred million million million) planets in the universe which contain sentient beings - a living universe indeed!.

The mistake that many scientists make when they consider the question about life elsewhere is that they are really thinking about whether there is *earthly* life elsewhere. Life does not require a planet with water, oxygen, etc, since these are the conditions for *earthly* life. It is no coincidence that the Earth's environment is ideal for life on earth since the life that we observe around us evolved to suit the prevailing conditions (if the theory of evolution is true). In other words, if the conditions on Earth were very different it would still be possible to argue: "if Earthly conditions were any different to how they are life might never have evolved".

Earthly life requires earthly conditions;
but alien life requires alien conditions.

I found it amusing, but sad at the same time, the way that scientists tested for life on the moon - (if it is true that man has indeed landed on the moon, and there is considerable evidence that he hasn't) - they supposedly set up equipment to test for the output of carbon dioxide, since all life *on earth* respires by taking in Oxygen and giving out Carbon Dioxide. This is true of both animals and plants although the latter undergo photosynthesis as well. How ridiculous to expect life to respire on the moon the same way as life on earth, if it evolved in such different conditions. All that this test showed (apart from how short-sighted scientists can be) is that there is no *Earthly life* on the moon, i.e. no life that releases energy by taking in oxygen and giving out carbon dioxide. Obvious really! How could anyone be stupid enough to expect otherwise?

If sentient beings which evolved in an atmosphere of chlorine gas and extremely hot conditions were brought to the Earth, they would probably die immediately they took 1 breath in our atmosphere, and they would find the Sahara desert inhospitably cold. This is not as hypothetical as you may think since the bacteria found in volcanic larva can only survive at extremely high temperatures, if they are brought into what we consider a hospitable environment, they perish. So in our search for life elsewhere we certainly do not need to look for "Earthly" conditions.

Before ending this section I would like to explain a common scientific theory that many scientists believe about how the "death" of the universe will come about. What *death* means in this context is the cessation of all activity.

Thermodynamic theory tells us that when two objects at different temperatures interact, there is a flow of energy from the hot body to the cold one, and this energy flow will continue until the two objects reach the same temperature. This theory tells us that the universe is slowly "unwinding" or running down - as hot objects such as stars get cooler, and cold objects such as planets get warmer, there will eventually come a time when everything in the universe will be at the same temperature and then energy transfers can no longer take place, the universe will be totally inactive for if no energy transfers can take place then nothing can happen. In scientific circles this is known as "the heat death of the universe". The problem with this idea is that it doesn't include life as a property of the universe - science has omitted to include consciousness as part of the universe. As I have explained, this narrow scientific viewpoint sees life as an improbable accident that randomly occurs in a dead mechanistic universe.

One possible hypothesis to counter this mechanistic viewpoint is that while this thermodynamic unwinding is taking place there is a constant flow of energy occurring and life is present all over the universe to intercept this energy as it flows. So, life is continuously evolving to ever increasing energy states - in other words, as the material universe unwinds, life everywhere is balancing this with a corresponding "winding up". This wound up, fully charged consciousness has infinite potential and therefore the ability to do *anything* and may start the whole cycle again discharging it's energy into the manifest universe making stars and planets all over again (I wonder if this whole process might take six days with a rest period on the seventh day?) This is only one hypothesis - one of many possible alternatives. The point that I would like to emphasise is that any world view which doesn't include consciousness as a fundamental property of the universe must, inevitably, lead to dubious conclusions.

I believe that a wholistic viewpoint on any subject such as cosmology, physics, biology, philosophy, etc, must include some aspect of the invisible realm such as spirit or consciousness. Most importantly "spirit" must be an essential part of our mindset if we are at all interested in personal growth.

To become more spiritual means to become more in touch with that deeper (or higher) part of ourselves. To enhance our spirituality we must let go of many attachments and we must also be willing to let go of self-imposed limiting beliefs. Let us now consider in more detail what it actually means to be more spiritual, how this contrasts from religious attachment, and most importantly how we can remove the blocks which stop us being in touch with our spirituality .

Becoming more Spiritual

THE POWER OF PRAYER

Whatever you desire,
when you pray, believe that you shall receive it,
and you shall have it.
MARK 12, 24.

The word "prayer" is often used in the general sense of any communication with God or some divinity or higher energy source. The communication can take the form of speaking, listening, asking for help or advice, or giving thanks. The two main uses of the word prayer that I shall consider are:

1) When a request is made of God, the universe, the creative energy, or whatever "power" is believed in.

2) When thanks is given for the prayer coming true - even before it has. This is the most powerful form of prayer.

When you thank God in advance for that which
you choose to experience in your reality, you,
in effect, acknowledge that it is there.
NEALE DONALD WALSCH

Listening usually requires silence and this is closer to meditation than prayer. It is often said that Prayer is speaking to God, whereas meditation is listening to God.

A prayer can be a form of suggestion but instead of saying it to yourself you can project it onto an outside force. For example if you are suffering from tension and feeling in disharmony, you can use the technique of self-suggestion and repeat to yourself many times over and over again: "I am now feeling a deep sense of inner peace". If however, you are religious and believe that God can help you then you could say: "Please God, give me inner peace". Either statement may lead to the same result if we believe *and expect* it to since our thoughts are powerful enough to bring about, through our consciousness, the manifestation of our reality.

For what one thinks, that he becomes -
this is the mystery of eternity.
MAITRI UPANISHAD

It isn't necessary to believe in a personal God who is listening the way that a man may be listening, in order to pray for something. A religious person may say "If you have faith then your prayers will be answered", well this may be true even if you don't believe in a personal God. This may be the case for one of three reasons:
1) Your mind is powerful enough to create whatever you truly believe.
2) The universe responds to your expectations.
3) Consciousness itself is the most powerful force in the universe, and as soon as you hold something powerfully and vividly in your consciousness you create a cosmic blue-print that begins to change the universe before you even act. It might be that this energy within all things that permeates the universe and connects everything, responds to our hopes and expectations, and in this way our consciousness creates our reality.

A prayer can truly work wonders, the important thing is to believe that your prayer will work, and it will. In other words, **even if you are agnostic, you can still pray!** From the contents of the previous sections you may understand that at the deepest levels *our consciousness is God,* and therefore, according to this viewpoint, prayer is fairly similar to affirmations.

Another way of explaining what is going on when prayer works, is to say that, through prayer we may tap into an energy within the universe to achieve whatever we are praying for. One way of describing this, is to consider that our consciousness impinges on

63

and makes its mark on the universal field which we are immersed in. Our thoughts affect this field and what manifests in the universe or materialises in our lives is a result of this field. Since we are all one, it is not simply that our consciousness affects the universal energy field - *it is* the field. If you can accept that this is the case then it is no wonder that our life is a manifestation of our consciousness.

> *For what is prayer,*
> *but the expansion of yourself into the living ether?*
> KAHLIL GIBRAN

As I explain in my book *You are what you think*, creating our reality involves three factors - desire, belief and expectation. It is the latter that is most powerful and when you expect something without any contemplation of doubt then the blueprint formed by the power of your consciousness (or God's) begins to bring it into being - for this reason the second form of prayer - giving thanks - is the most powerful. This form of prayer holds a positive expectation of the result yet with a peaceful acceptance of the outcome.

> *If we want to manifest something in our lives,*
> *we first have to be convinced that we can.*

Whatever is the reality of *how* prayer works, I think that the most self-empowering stance to take is to feel that we can use either prayers or affirmations to manifest whatever we want in our lives, but we must believe in whatever method we use, for it to be effective.

The belief in a helpful, personal God is sometimes a very useful concept for someone to believe in. For example, if someone has a lack of confidence regarding what they are able to achieve using their own inner resources, and they have a strong faith in

God and what "He" can do, then prayer can be a very useful aid in their life.

Obviously, the disadvantageous aspects of prayer is that sometimes one may request something of God, sit back and just hope for it to come. Although it may be true that much of what manifests in our life may be a result of faith, trust and positive expectation, there is also a very valid argument that we must take positive action if we want positive results.

> *Prayer indeed is good,*
> *but while calling on the Gods*
> *a man should himself lend a hand.*
> HIPPOCRATES

RELIGION AND SPIRITUALITY

There is a great contrast between religion and spirituality. A spiritual person is someone who has the quest of getting in touch with their essence, to find a deeper meaning to everything, and to become at one with the universe. Religious people are occasionally spiritual but not always since true spirituality requires an openness to life. A religious person is usually someone who has attached to a certain system of belief, with rules set out by a church or some other religious figurehead. The attachment to a doctrine can, at times, be very destructive since it tends to close the minds of the individual that holds to it.

> *True spirituality is beyond rule and ritual,*
> *or attachment to labels or doctrine.*

The word religion comes from the Latin "Re legare" which means "to relate (or connect) completely". The true aim of all religions is to discover *truth* by making connection with the ultimate source of life and in so doing, enhance the more divine states of the soul - honesty, appreciation of beauty, heightened awareness, integrity, joy, and of course, love.

The deepest principles of most religions are very spiritual, but as they are passed down through the generations they become more and more corrupted. Remember, any chain is only as strong as its weakest link, and so, if the "truth" is passed down by word of mouth, or if a translation is carried out on the information, then the interpretation is only as accurate or profound as the least wise person in the chain.

> *A Chinese whisper*
> *always gives the Wong reply.*
> NOLAN JOHN

Many of the great religions of the world have always taught that we have the ultimate truth within us. The problems have come into the religions when men who are not "connected" try to explain God's will.

> *Religion became corrupted when leaders were assigned to*
> *explain God's will to people instead of showing them*
> *how to find this direction within themselves.*
> JAMES REDFIELD/CAROL ADRIENNE

I would like to emphasise that I have a lot of respect for many of the principles that great men such as Buddha and Jesus taught, however, this is in great contrast to the teachings of the church which is simply an institution run by men who propound many ideas based on their own interpretations. Some of these ideas are useful and help followers to live more spiritual lives, but many ideas are ridiculous and have, through the ages, caused far more harm than good. The history of the world holds on record innumerable wars which have occurred in the name of religion. If someone can kill in the name of religion, or even argue and insult someone who disagrees with their views, then they are totally missing the point of the religion and attaching to superficial, corrupt dogmas propounded by "men of the church".

> *Organised religion sometimes pulls us away from the spiritual part of who we are.*
> *SUSAN JEFFERS*

Compare two Christians: One who is always talking about going to church, how Jesus died to save us for our sins and the importance of holy communion or other rituals, and another who never talks about religion but *lives by the principles of what Jesus taught*, helping whoever he can and spreading love with every opportunity that arises. Unfortunately, in all religions the majority of followers are more like the first than the second. Many followers tend to attach to the superficial aspects of the religion, such as names, labels, life stories, and so on, and they overlook the deepest principles of the religion. They are keener to say: "I belong to this religion" or "I will kill anyone who says anything against my religion", than to say: "I believe that we should all live lovingly" or "We should refrain from behaviour which causes harm to others".

A religion should give its followers two things:
1)   Feelings of goodwill and friendliness towards all humanity, and a way of living which helps one to better serve his fellow citizen.
2)   A greater sense of inner peace, an enhanced appreciation of life and a greater feeling of happiness and contentment.

If you are religious, and your religion does not achieve these two objectives, or if it instils guilt, fear, worry, anger or causes arguments with those who are not of the same religion then I would suggest that your life would be much better if you were to drop the religion and try to discover the truth by opening up your mind to the lessons taught by life itself.

> *True religion is to cleanse oneself with*
> *pure thoughts, pure words, and pure deeds.*
> ZOROASTRIANISM

If you are religious and you want to live by "Gods word" the important thing is not just to talk about and to think about God, it is to try and live by the deepest principles of what your religion teaches. Just as thinking about food cannot satisfy your physical hunger, simply thinking about God will not satisfy your spiritual hunger. It is by connecting with God, or the energy of the universe, that you will receive most spiritual sustenance and, for most people, this is just as likely to be achieved while sitting in a beautiful park than while participating in a church mass on a Sunday morning.

If you are interested in the deepest principles of what Jesus and Buddha taught, then I would highly recommend the series of books by Baird T. Spalding called *The Life and Teachings of the masters of the far East* published by Devorss Publications. In Volume Two, Spalding explains in a very clear way that religious devotees need to *idealise* not *idolise;* about Jesus he explained:

> *He is idolised by a majority of*
> *your people, and that is where they err.*
> *Instead of the Idol he should be the Ideal.*
> BAIRD T. SPALDING

If Jesus was alive today (and maybe he is) I am certain that he wouldn't want to be idolised, he would be more interested in how you live - to live by the ideals of what he taught.

TRANSCEND RELIGIOUS DOGMA

Don't hold an attachment to any one religion,
since he who knows only one, knows none.

There's a subtle distinction between transcending as opposed to rejecting. We need to work on transcending certain belief systems, without rejecting them. To reject a religion means to close your mind to any of its teachings, and in so doing turn your back on the possibility of gaining useful insights from the teaching. To transcend religious dogma means to not attach to the teachings with the attitude that *this is the way,* since this has the effect of closing the door to truth.

Live as lamps to yourselves,
as refuges to yourselves,
with no other refuges.
THE BUDDHA

Many religious teachings put forward the unfortunate dogma that it is unhelpful or even dangerous to ask too many questions. They may teach that "you should just *have faith* in what you are told regarding this religion but *be careful* about delving into, or exploring other ideas". This dogma keeps the disciples or followers from finding wisdom since *blind* faith stops the healthy, open, questioning attitude, which is necessary if we are to ever discover "the truth".

Faith without doubt is folly!
THOMAS ALLEN

In religion, the word faith is used in two ways, sometimes it is taken to mean "an unquestioning belief", while at other times it means "an unfailing trust". Whereas to have great faith and trust in yourself, in your abilities, and in life is a very positive quality, if by faith we mean "an unquestioning belief" then it is not positive at all. This type of blind faith is very unhealthy, since we can only discover "the truth" if we questioningly doubt rather than if we unquestioningly believe. As soon as the questioning attitude stops, the chance of gaining wisdom ceases.

> *There is the most interesting resemblance*
> *between the effects of stimulants, narcotics*
> *or hypnotic control, and blind unreasoning faith.*
> *The latter also benumbs and paralyses*
> *judgement and reason.*
> HENRY LINDLAHR

So, to believe anything unquestioningly is a very negative and dangerous characteristic, and therefore it is never acceptable to take the statement from anyone: "just have faith", since this is another way of saying "don't think about it, just believe it!". This dogma is propounded to keep the masses following a religion which if they thought about more deeply, they would come to realise how full of errors and inconsistencies it is. The questioning attitude is repressed for the convenience of the church authorities.

> *If you do have faith, let it be not blind faith,*
> *but a faith that glows with wisdom.*
> ANDREA PHOTIOU

The path to wisdom is through doubt; blind faith only leads to ignorance. While growing up we question many rules - those questions are totally healthy and a necessary part of learning about the world and the best way to behave. But if we hear a certain statement or rule enough times, then even if it isn't very sensible we start to just accept it and go along with it. The western educational system perpetuates this sad state of affairs.

Do not blindly believe what others say.
See for yourself what brings contentment, clarity, and peace.
That is the path for you to follow.
THE BUDDHA

So, we must give careful consideration to every idea that we hear and decide without clinging onto our previous conditioning or "education" whether it is a sensible and useful belief to take on board. I put the word education in inverted commas because in reality most conventional education is actually a mis-education or indoctrination into a set of beliefs which are set up by the system in order to control the masses.

Public opinion is a permeating influence,
and it exacts obedience to itself;
it requires us to think other men's thoughts,
to speak other men's words,
to follow other men's habits.
WALTER BAGEHOT

When a belief starts to become fairly widespread, many people take it on board simply because everyone else has! This is a common occurrence but one which can be transcended with awareness. Only believe what you think is right, not what others tell you is right, and only behave in ways that you feel in your heart is right, not what others tell you is right.

Believe those who are seeking the truth;
Doubt those who find it.
ANDRE GIDE

71

People *attaching* to any system of belief can hold onto dogmas without realising it - this is true not only of religious followers but also of academic or intellectual types such as scientists, psychologists and doctors.

> *Be as a lamp unto them that walk in darkness.*
> THE BAHA'I FAITH

There are scientific dogmas (e.g. the big bang theory and the theory of relativity), there are social dogmas (e.g. Our brain is the source of consciousness, milk is good for the health, man has been to the moon), there are medical dogmas (antibiotics save lives, germs cause disease, vaccinations reduce the risk of serious illness, AIDS is caused by the HIV virus, fluoride is good for the teeth), and so on. I am not saying that all of these beliefs are wrong, (although, I do *doubt* most of them), what I am saying is that they are all based on *assumptions* and if the assumptions are wrong then the beliefs that they are based on are very likely to be wrong also.

> *The great majority of us follow the prevailing orthodoxy,*
> *without ever asking ourselves whether this*
> *choice might actually be right for us.*
> LIZ HODGKINSON

I have met scientists who are so "attached" to their scientific world view that they are unable to see or hear other points of view which are not consistent with their intellectual framework.

> *It is in overcoming self-doubt that we will develop*
> *the independence of mind to doubt every*
> *so-called truth that we are told.*

If we have a certain independence of mind we come to realise that "to obey" we must trust the "authority" that is giving the orders or setting the rules. And once we realise that all "authorities" are just people doing their job or living out their own mission then we may see that it is not always wise to "just have faith". Indeed most people in authority are not living their mission but simply doing as they're told by those who run the system.

> *It wasn't sin that was born*
> *on the day when Eve picked an apple;*
> *what was born on that day was a splendid*
> *virtue called disobedience.*
> ORIANA FALLACI

It is harmful if our trust comes from blind faith, respect and trust are two qualities that need to be earned. Maybe God hadn't yet earned Eve's trust when he told her to leave the apple alone, or maybe he didn't explain why she shouldn't have it, and so she did the right thing and tried it!

> *...the irony of all this is that*
> *I do not want your worship,*
> *I do not need your obedience,*
> *and it is not necessary for you to serve me.*
> GOD
> (VIA NEALE DONALD WALSCH)

Disobedience is, indeed, a splendid virtue, since it is this that leads us to new territory and often great discoveries. We must realise that to gain knowledge which will enable us to release our true potential it is essential not to just believe what we are told simply because those who are telling us have "credentials" or wear a white coat, or have some important positions in authority.

In fact these are the people who we should most doubt since they are likely to be the ones who are the most indoctrinated (or *mis*-educated).

The only way to discover real knowledge which may lead you to "truth" is to go in search of information with an independent, questioning and doubting mind. **The only true education is a self-education.**

> *In a world of prejudice and rampant irrationality,*
> *of opinion manipulation and standardised attitudes,*
> *of ideological indoctrination and occult persuasions;*
> *nothing is more needed than an independent,*
> *critical and clear mind.*
> PIERO FERRUCCI

THE FEAR OF GOD
IS THE END OF WISDOM

One of the most harmful religious teachings is that of an angry, judgmental God. If you feel the need to attach to the concept of a personal God, then it is much healthier if it is one who is for you and not against you - a non-judgmental, loving, compassionate God. The attachment to the concept of a vengeful, angry God can cause only harm, and the fear produced by believing in this ridiculous concept is the cause of a whole host of internal, psychological problems.

> *The false gods stand most visibly*
> *and scream the loudest: "I am the one".*
> *The false gods tend to use fear to control the flock.*
> STEPHEN PARKHILL

If someone lives with the constant feeling that this judgmental God is looking over their shoulder, and they then "sin", the fear can produce a whole host of psychosomatic conditions. I include the word *sin* in inverted commas because many religious followers are conditioned to believe that much of their behaviour is sinful even if it does no harm to any living creature.

A God who judges and rewards or punishes,
based on how good he feels about what you've been up to
is a simplistic view of God, based on your mythology.
It has nothing to do with who I am.
GOD.
(VIA NEALE DONALD WALSCH)

If you are religious, and have had a fear-based conditioning, maybe God can help you to transcend some of the more negative aspects of your indoctrination by using the power of prayer and affirmation. Try repeating many times any of the following:

1)   God never judges what I do but oversees with compassion, love and understanding.

2)   God is loving and good and always works *for* me to help me in every situation.

3)   With God's love, I can achieve absolutely anything that I want to achieve in life.

4)   God, please help me to be open and receptive to alternative ways of seeing the world.

To be ruled by fear is destructive in every respect. We need to learn to trust that life is on our side and most importantly to be motivated by love rather than by fear.

FEAR IS A PRISON;
LOVE IS FREEDOM

Fear is the energy which contracts, closes down,
draws in, runs, hides, hoards, harms.
Love is the energy which expands, opens up,
sends out, stays, reveals, shares, heals.
NEALE DONALD WALSCH

Fear is talked about so much, as is love, but these two words are very rarely defined, maybe it is because they are almost undefinable. The best way to develop a deeper understanding of these two words/concepts is by discussion - which is the purpose of this section. My intention is to analyse these words and hopefully gain some insights and inspire the reader to develop not only a greater understanding but more importantly to move towards a higher level of awareness which will enable fear and other negative emotions to be replaced by love and other positive emotions. Are they emotions? Are they states of mind? Are they states of being?

Let's begin by looking at a few words in common use, along with their opposites:

Love - Hate
Trust - Fear
Respect/Admiration - Judgement
Connection - separation

You may think some of these words are totally unrelated and have little to do with the heading of this section but I hope my reasons for their inclusion will become clear as we go through their meanings.

76

Love versus hate: Most people would say that the opposite to love is hate, in this context love means "to like very much" and hate means "to dislike very much". This is not at all the definition of love that I am seeking.

Trust versus fear: To trust in life means to have a relaxed, peaceful feeling due to an inner knowing that things will work out well. To fear life means to have a "dreadful expectation" that terrible things are going to happen. In fact the word fear is often taken to be an acronym (F.E.A.R.) for Fantasised Expectations Appearing Real. I think that this is getting closer to what fear is.

Fear is a perversion of the great law of faith;
it is faith in evil.
HENRY LINDLAHR

Respect versus judgement: To respect or admire someone means to put your focus on their positive qualities. To pass judgement on someone is to focus on their negative characteristics. In reality I believe that admiration or judgement are actually statements about the person who is doing the admiring or judging and not really about the person who is being admired or judged.

Connection versus separation! Why did I include these words in this section? I believe that these are the concepts which can bring our understanding together. True love means connection. When you feel connected to life this is when you truly love life and when you are able to trust without a sense of fear.

The mind thinks;
Love links.
CHRISTOPHER GILMORE

77

You connect by withholding judgement and instead by putting attention on beauty. Observation of beauty is a way of establishing a connection between your essence and the object of beauty. When you observe the beauty of nature you become connected to it and move into the state of love. When you put your attention onto the beauty of a person, you are also establishing a connection which moves you into the state of love.

> *The essence of love isn't a feeling*
> *- it is a state of being.*
> DR. DEEPAK CHOPRA

Separation or isolation gives rise to the opposite state that I have just described. When you put your attention upon perceived ugliness you move into the judgmental state which creates a separation between you and the object of perception. In reality the "ugliness" isn't really there at all - the perception of ugliness is within the consciousness of the observer and has come about due to the state of separateness (from universal consciousness).

> *I will judge no-one today.*
> *I would rather be cheated once or twice*
> *than live my whole life in fear and suspicion.*
> MIKE LIPKIN

When we feel separated - me against the rest of the universe - we become isolated from the source of love which permeates the whole universe.

I didn't explain this in the section God and Man but I believe that the universal consciousness, or God, is actually pure love. When we connect with this, we live in *a blissful state of love* and when we are separate from it we live in *a nightmarish state of fear*.

Fear is the negative destructive force
which directs our faith power towards the
manifestation of our nightmares.
MIKE PENDRAGON

When we feel separate we hate, when we feel separate we judge, and most importantly **when we feel separate we live in a constant state of fear.** If, by harbouring negative emotions and holding a negative attitude towards life, we become separated from our essence (same as universal consciousness) then we will inevitably live in a state of fear.

Fear clings to and clutches all that we have;
love gives all that we have away.
Fear holds close, love holds dear.
Fear grasps; love lets go.
NEALE DONALD WALSCH

So if you want to release fear and *become* love the most important step you can take is to "become connected" - I will suggest a few techniques on how to do this in the section *Practical steps to enlightenment.*

There is the path of fear and the path of love.
Which will you follow?
THE BUDDHA

SEXUALITY AND SPIRITUALITY

Spirituality must also be sensuous,
because a spiritual person is one who lives fully
in the moment, which means living fully in the body.
DR. DEEPAK CHOPRA

The fact that sex is a taboo subject in our society is mainly because of the Christian roots of our culture where the religious teachings put forward a view of sex as something dirty and immoral. Many, many people within our society, not only those with a religious background, are brought up to believe that their genitals are dirty (urine, by the way, is a completely germ free, sterile liquid) and that the naked body is something to be ashamed of. They are also taught that the sex act is "naughty" or immoral, in fact within religious circles it is often given labels with negative connotations such as "fornication". Many religious institutions, not only Christianity, propound that you should feel guilty about your sexuality, they equate sex with sin and this includes not only sexual activity but even thoughts and feelings about sex. How can an act of procreation be seen as such a sin?

Life is the result of a Big Bang!
NOLAN JOHN

Many religious teachers put an unhealthy emphasis on the sinfulness of their followers in order to encourage feelings of guilt which must then be dealt with by repenting for their sins - what nonsense! A religious upbringing which equates sex with sin can dampen sexual enjoyment enormously and may cause many sexual problems within a relationship.

Negative conditioning doesn't stop you
from engaging in the sex act;
it just stops you enjoying it!

Obviously the sex act can be immoral - rape, sexual abuse, or any type of unconsented sex - but religious authorities have caused immense damage in history by equating sexual feelings with immorality. The suppression of our sexuality will only create problems.

*If the creative energy is suppressed, by the
suppression of sexual feelings and natural talent, its power
becomes imbalanced. This will manifest in other ways
- through violence, rape, crime, wars and depression.
More spiritual sex = less global violence!*
DAVID ICKE

Of course, it is very important to live morally, but what is morality? I define morality as behaviour which causes no intentional harm to any living creature, and conversely immorality is behaviour which *needlessly* causes harm to another living creature. So, if we use this definition, who do you think is living more immorally: A prostitute who spends her day giving pleasure to many people, or a priest who preaches about the sinfulness of "the desires of the flesh" creating guilt and other negative emotions in his congregation? Since immorality is behaviour which doesn't hurt anyone, it can be said that a priest who causes suffering by preaching the sinfulness of the sex act, is far *more immoral* than a prostitute who has sex for a living and is doing no harm to anyone! A similar argument could be used against the police - when the police raid a brothel, they are committing a highly immoral act against a group of women who are providing what could be considered to be a highly valuable service to society, and instead of being rewarded they are being punished. Maybe prostitution is one of the most honourable professions that there is! (It is certainly one of the oldest).

I will repeat the question above, relating it to the police. Who do you think is living more immorally? A prostitute who earns her money by giving pleasure to many people, or the police who arrest the prostitutes and therefore earn their money by causing pain? To me, the answer is obvious.

I am certainly not advocating prostitution, and I believe that sex should actually unite body, mind and soul. However, each of us must live our own path while developing at our own rate, and to see prostitution as a crime is as ridiculous as to see working in a baker's shop as a crime. (Bakery products are a major cause of disease, by the way, but this is another subject!)

Apart from causing guilt and inhibitions in the followers of the religion, I am sure that much of the bad behaviour of the repressed followers has been caused by the frustration of being forced to go against their basic nature. I wonder how many catholic confessions are about feelings of guilt because of sexual thoughts or behaviour where no immorality is involved. It is ridiculous and very damaging to propound that thinking about sex is immoral since it doesn't harm anyone. This is such a destructive, negative view and has probably caused so much grief throughout history that it must be true to say that the religious teaching is itself far more immoral than the sex act!

> *Our families, peers, society and religious organisations*
> *only aid us in attempting to suppress, control*
> *or exploit what is natural.*
> SHAKTI GAWAIN

Those who have had an upbringing with lots of negative conditioning regarding sex usually have a similar negative conditioning regarding masturbation as well. A Catholic priest once told me that a substantial number of confessions that he has listened to were related to guilt about sexual feelings - particularly masturbation.

> *Masturbation: the primary sexual activity of mankind.*
> *In the nineteenth century it was a disease;*
> *in the twentieth it's a cure.*
> THOMAS SZASZ

Considerable research has been done in recent years on the relationship between sex and health. Contrary to the old-fashioned view that too much sex or masturbation is bad for the health, studies have shown that those with an active sex life or regular sexual release are healthier and live longer than those who feel ashamed of, or repress, their sexuality. It has also been found that affectionate, loving sex is good for the heart and can neutralise the harmful effects on the health of sorrow and grief .

Sexual exchange with a loving partner
promotes feelings of well-being and builds self-esteem.
JUDITH SACHS.

According to American health expert Judith Sachs, sex can enhance your immune system, cure your insomnia, eliminate stress, relieve pain, ease stiffness and even cure your headaches. Knowing this, feeling stressed or having a headache should motivate us to have sex rather than avoid it!

Many of the beneficial effects of sex are related to the orgasm and so some sexual therapists claim that it doesn't matter too much if it is with a partner or by yourself - this only matters, if you feel that it matters. The orgasm is a discharge for all kinds of tension, and immediately after orgasm a hormone called Serotonin is released which helps to induce deep relaxation and sleep. Also during orgasm the brain releases endorphins which are the body's natural pain killers - in this way, good sex helps to relieve pain.

From a common sense point of view, receiving pleasure from the stimulation of the genitals is no more immoral than receiving pleasure from the stimulation of the taste buds by eating something sweet - but not many religious followers would say that enjoying a cake is immoral! Obviously, as in all the pleasures of life, over-indulgence can be a problem. However, if

83

we are going to argue about self-indulgence and self-abuse, it is a fact that eating an artificial sweet, cake or biscuit is just as self-indulgent as masturbation and is certainly more of an abuse on the body. Regarding the effects on the health I think that it is true to say that for women the only adverse effect of masturbation is a possible depletion of energy, and this is more likely to be the case if there is guilt and shame involved. So, for women especially, consuming unnatural sweets or cakes simply for the pleasurable stimulation of the taste buds is probably more of a self-abuse than a self-generated orgasm. However, for men it is important to be aware that semen is a valuable source of minerals such as zinc, selenium, and so on, and is also high in protein, so *excessive* masturbation can cause a mineral and amino acid depletion which may have various side effects, one being baldness. Maybe that old wives tale that *too much* masturbation causes baldness may have a little truth after all. And possibly this is one of the reasons why men generally suffer from baldness more than women. But please notice my emphasis on the words "too much" - and this obviously applies to sex as well as masturbation.

Wilhelm Reich, an assistant of Sigmund Freud, believed that the orgasm was a way of tapping into the source of the life-energy, which could help us along our path of spiritual development. He put a lot of importance on the orgasm as a release of, not only sexual tension, but also pent-up feelings and inhibitions.

Sex also helps considerably to relieve menstrual pains if a women has sex during the few days leading up to her period. Severe menstrual pains may be linked to repressed sexuality - women who suffer from the worst period pains often have negative conditioning related to masturbation or guilty feelings about their sexuality. This guilt can be eliminated with good counselling, therapy or self-hypnosis.

To emphasis how ridiculous it is for a religion to teach that masturbation is an unnatural and sinful activity, imagine a religious cult that teaches "drinking water is a sin", and "it is *immoral* to drink anything in public". You may think that no-one could believe such a ridiculous teaching but if you were born into a culture where everyone stated this "truth" and you never saw anyone drink because *it's such an embarrassing thing to do,* then you may begin to believe it. The result of this would be that because of our nature everyone would still occasionally drink particularly when they are thirsty. But if this belief permeated our society then nobody would ever drink in public, everyone would drink in secret, and many people would feel guilty and ashamed of the fact that they sometimes can't resist a drink! They may even feel embarrassed about the fact that they sometimes feel thirsty. At confession they may state "I'm sorry father I felt thirsty today and I couldn't stop thinking about water".

Sex, including masturbation is very much like this. I wonder how many nuns, priests and religious followers suffer from this type of guilt and shame when they just think about sex or masturbate, because their religion teaches them to feel bad about their sexuality. This is just as crazy as being taught that drinking water is a sin. In fact, the whole religious institution would be so much more acceptable (and moral) if it acknowledged the sexuality of every human being and didn't try to suppress the sexuality of "Gods people". It would certainly stop a lot of the homosexuality that goes on in convents and monasteries (not that there is anything wrong with homosexuality between consenting, homosexual adults), if the monks and nuns were encouraged to feel that masturbation is normal.

I once had a girlfriend (a Christian) who denied that she ever masturbated, but after I told her about all the girls I have previously known who also said that and then eventually "owned

85

up", she said that she "occasionally" did too!

I find it hard to believe that the vast, incredible Intelligence that created this entire Universe is only an old man sitting on a cloud above the planet Earth..........watching my genitals!
LOUISE L. HAY

We all have a considerable amount of subconscious programming related to sex, and for many of us, much of this is detrimental to our general health and well-being. Our quality of life would be enhanced considerably if we could transcend any negative conditioning about sex, for our sexuality is an integral part of what we are and to deny this cannot be conducive to finding inner peace and happiness.

Many people still suffer from the mistaken idea that spiritual energy and sexual energy are opposite, instead of recognising that they are the same force.
SHAKTI GAWAIN

To pursue this argument a little further, it might be true to say that an orgasm may bring you closer to God. One of the keys to living life to the full is learning to live fully in the moment. Most people would agree that the time when it is easiest to "give yourself to the moment" is during an orgasm. Maybe at this moment we are experiencing our oneness with the divine.

The orgasm may be one of the many pathways to God.

In great contrast to the Christian view, the Indian religious traditions such as tantrism see sex as a deeply spiritual activity and a pathway to the divine. Rather than associate sex with sin they connect it with divinity and teach that a man can only attain

86

spiritual completeness through physical union with a women and so sexual intercourse is seen as a highly spiritual act. In fact, in the temples of India, prostitution holds no stigma and is a highly respected profession - what profession could be more spiritual than one where every day you are giving great pleasure to many people? What a contrast from the traditional christian view!

In the tantric religion they speak of sex as a spiritual activity as opposed to "the desire of the flesh", in fact, some express the view that God *is* sexual energy, and during an orgasm the energy of God is flowing through you. If this is true, then monks and nuns are making a big mistake remaining celibate and repressing their sexuality, since, in doing this they may be distancing themselves from God.

> *Sex is the gateway to life.*
> FRANK HARRIS

The Prophet Krishna was said to have given great pleasure to more than 16,000 women during his life on earth - this was never regarded with disapproval, on the contrary it was seen as a measure of how much love he had to give. This is probably going a bit too far for most of us who have had a typical western conditioning. The tantric and the christian views on sex are two opposite extremes and I believe that we should endeavour to find a balance between these two viewpoints.

> *Masturbation is mastering the turbulence.*
> NOLAN JOHN

To illustrate what sexual beings we are, it is interesting to consider that over the planet as a whole, every hour approximately *forty million* men and women have an orgasm which means that in the time it takes you to say the word "orgasm", over eleven thousand people have had one!

CELIBACY AND ABSTINENCE

I would like to emphasise at this point that I do not advocate casual sex and promiscuity. My aim in writing the previous section is to help the reader feel relaxed about their sexual feelings and their sexuality. Although, I would always endeavour to withhold judgement from someone who does enjoy free sex, it is certainly not something which I would advocate.

Sex is an expression of love which is meant to stimulate the soul as well as the genitals.

I believe that to reach higher levels of spirituality, chastity can be a very useful tool and that all types of *indulgence* are better avoided - this includes smoking, alcohol, junk food, chocolate and meaningless entertainment, as well as sex. However, I want to emphasise the importance of letting go of feelings of guilt. Sexual feelings are a natural consequence of being human and to acknowledge this is essential before we can rise to higher levels of spirituality.

With love being an all engulfing essence of so many aspects of living well, the part that sex plays in it should be akin to all creative expressions.
ANDREA PHOTIOU

Although there are arguments to support the fact that an orgasm may be good for the health, this, however, might not be the case if the orgasm is obtained from casual or inappropriate partners. The consequences of careless promiscuity can be fairly severe - venereal diseases, unwanted pregnancy, emotional turmoil, and so on. (I didn't include AIDS as one of the consequences since, contrary to popular opinion, this is not a sexually transmissible disease).

Sometimes, a promiscuous person may not just be searching for sexual satisfaction, but may be searching for love, and in this situation casual sex can very often lead to emotional pain, since their search for love really comes from a need to feel whole and this emotional insecurity can often lead to the wrong choices of sexual partners.

For some, sex is an addictive desire. As with all addictive desires, if it is not satisfied the result is misery, frustration, boredom, anger, or some other negative emotion, and if it is satisfied, there will still be the need for more. Once sex becomes an addictive desire then it is not possible to get enough.

As far as sexual relationships are concerned, the healthiest way is to follow your heart not your hormones, i.e. to do what you feel within you is right, according to your own principles - and nobody else's. Keeping in mind that sexual frustration might not be good for the physical, emotional or mental health, whereas sexual release is, if a loving partner is unavailable then some kind of release might be advisable, and the safest, most moral way is through masturbation.

NUTRITION AND SPIRITUALITY

This is a subject which is often neglected by many who get on to the spiritual path. There is considerable evidence that feelings of inner peace, harmony, love and other positive emotions enhance our health. Conversely, our health has a profound effect on how easily we can connect to our spirit. It is also true that the less healthy one is the greater the tendency towards irritability, nervousness, insecurity, and many other negative emotions. It is now very well established that the quality of food we eat has a profound effect on our health and general state of well being.

Most people who get on the spiritual path and develop the desire to get in touch with their spiritual side to become more loving and peaceful, generally concentrate on developing the following habits:

1) Daily meditation
2) Forgiveness practice
3) Observation and contemplation of beauty.

These are wonderful and useful practices, however, I believe that in isolation they are of very limited benefit. In other words, if the soul is residing in a toxic body then heightened states of consciousness become extremely difficult, if not impossible, to attain.

It is a sad fact that for most people, diet is ignored as an essential consideration. Many religious texts do, however, put minor emphasis on the avoidance of meat, saying that it may produce bad karma and that it has a "low vibration" and so can pull you down into courser levels of consciousness. But in most texts on spirituality very little is usually said about the importance of avoiding other unnatural foods which the human body is not designed to consume. There are presently a few books on the market which go into the connection between nutrition and spirituality in greater detail than what I can deal with in this section, a wonderful book which I highly recommend is *Spiritual Nutrition and The Rainbow Diet* by Gabriel Cousens.

The essential point that I would like to put forward in this section is that **your inner state of peacefulness and harmony is greatly affected by the quality of blood flowing through your bloodstream.**

If your blood is pure your thoughts will be pure;
if your thoughts are pure you will attain
higher states of consciousness.

You may be aware that any experience that happens to you is not as important as your perception of that experience, your attitude to a problem is far more important than the problem itself. I believe that the secondary factor that influences our perceptions and attitude in any moment is our previous experiences, but the primary factor is the quality of the blood flowing through our veins.

> *Pure blood - not blue blood,*
> *is the mark of nobility.*
> NOLAN JOHN

We all know that many crimes are committed under the influence of alcohol and drugs but what is the most common drug that influences the behaviour of mankind. If we define a drug as any product that when flowing through the bloodstream has some adverse effect on behaviour, then I am convinced that the answer is "artificial food".

> *Whatever you put in your mouth and swallow*
> *influences the quality of blood flowing*
> *through your bloodstream.*

In fact there is mounting evidence that irritability, rage, nervous tension, clinical depression, and so on, are very strongly linked to nutritional deficiencies and junk food toxins flowing through the body. The main factor that is influencing how you feel at this very moment is the health of all the cells of your body, this in turn is determined by the quality of the blood that is flowing through your bloodstream. I believe that Irritability, rage and unreasonable reactions can often be instigated by poisons flowing through the blood stream. I am also convinced that selfishness and evil or violent, criminal behaviour has its *fundamental* cause in an unnatural diet. I emphasise "fundamental" because many criminals are so because they were brought up within a dysfunctional family. However, the only reason it was dysfunctional is because every member of the family were in a toxic, poisoned state.

Since nearly 100% of human beings are suffering from some level of bodily pollution this state of being appears totally normal, and so selfishness, irritability, and so on are seen as innate characteristics as opposed to unnatural states created by drugs, junk food poisons, toxins, or whatever.

Consider this hypothetical situation: A couple are sitting together romantically enjoying each other's company deeply in love. Then each of them is given a drug which causes extreme irritability. The slightest behaviour in each would be interpreted by the other as annoying, unreasonable, insulting, offensive, etc. They could have a flaming row, even physically assault each other all because of the drug flowing through their bloodstream. If they are unaware that they had been drugged they would each simply state that all their problems are the other one's fault. Ninety nine percent of couples in conflict say this - it's always the other one's fault!

In our society divorce is epidemic - it is now approaching 1 in 2. Why do most people get divorced? There are many reasons but the most common one is due to conflict which can't be resolved. However, the question that I find absolutely essential to ask is: "Does the conflict arise due to an intrinsic incompatibility between the two partners or is it because of the way each one responds during an argument about some trivial issue? Obviously it can be either or both but I believe that a very high percentage of divorces take place because of unreasonable behaviour. This is generally thought to be due to some undesirable characteristic of the individual which is unchangeable, but I believe it is because of the poisons flowing through the bloodstream.

Why is there so much scepticism in society about the obvious link between health and nutrition? It is because the degenerative effects of any particular foods we eat are very slow. It is like a man shut in a closed room with water dripping onto his head, he will eventually drown even though a drop of water doesn't seem to pose much of a threat. The effect of junk food is similar - the harmful effects of a bad diet don't manifest 1 day after eating a junk food meal. The effect is a slow, almost imperceptible, deterioration of health, which manifests first as a decrease in vitality, until eventually, if the bodies eliminatory efforts are suppressed, results in chronic illness. Whenever western man takes his "civilised" food to primitive people it usually takes about twenty years before chronic problems start to manifest, such as diabetes, osteoporosis, heart problems, bad jaw and teeth formation, etc

In fact, what I wrote in the previous paragraph: "the harmful effects of a bad diet don't manifest 1 day after eating a junk food meal" is not strictly true - the body always give us messages that something is not quite right the problem is that we usually misinterpret these messages. The statement that I should have made in the previous paragraph is that the *chronic* effects of a bad diet don't manifest immediately after eating a junk food meal. However, *there are* immediate effects since when we put poisons into our bloodstream it is impossible that there are no effects, it is just that the effects are not on what we would usually call "health" - the effects are on our mood, our concentration, our memory, our calmness of mind, and so on.

Human nature is perfection itself and all divergence from perfection is caused by inner pollution. The essence of human nature is beautiful and good and this inner beauty shines through when our soul is residing in a clean body. But there aren't many clean bodies in our society. Highly processed chemicalised food sold in supermarkets fill the bloodstream with unnatural chemicals.

So what is "junk food"? The answer to this question surprises many people since we live in a highly conditioned society where extremely unnatural foods are seen as normal. The worrying answer is that it is any food other than fresh, natural food which nature provided for us in their unprocessed form. The more a food is processed the worse it becomes. There are generally 2 categories of food processing:

1) Industrial or commercial food processing. E.g. refining, pasteurising, acidifying, artificially colouring and preserving, chemically enriching, flavouring, chlorinating, defatting, dehydrating, emulsifying, hydrogenating, nitrating, phosphating, etc. (believe it or not that is only a partial list!) This processing is carried out in order to:
   a) increase the shelf life of products, and
   b) produce items which are appealing to the eye and tongue.

2) Domestic food processing. These are generally thought to be harmless and indeed are far less destructive than the industrial processes outlined above. In order from the least to the most detrimental they are: cutting, chopping, grinding, mashing, juicing, liquidising, steaming, blanching, boiling, baking, fermenting, grilling, roasting, pressure cooking, frying and microwaving.

A natural diet consists of mainly natural foods eaten in their natural state, i.e. whole, fresh, uncooked fruits, lots of greens and other vegetables, unshelled fresh nuts and sprouted seeds.

Any foods which have been tampered with in any way cause inner pollution and lower our level of consciousness making us less spiritual than we may otherwise be. Artificial chemical foods may be at the root cause of all ill health, inner disharmony, and social problems.

The living cells of our body require living foods, there are no exceptions to this, our bodies can *survive* for a while on dead foods but they cannot *thrive* for any length of time. Once heat has been applied to the food it is no longer able to provide the same kind of nourishment since the cells of the food are no longer living. We can survive for a while on cooked foods but we can't thrive on them.

Living cells can only be nourished by living foods.

We thrive on fresh greens and fruit. In the past we may have needed to eat a few cooked grains or roots to sustain us through the winter months but this is no longer necessary. We are now in the privileged position that we can eat fruits and fresh vegetables all year round and thrive. Dead foods will only deplete our energy.

There are now many conclusive studies that show, irrefutably, that junk foods cause hyperactivity and behavioural problems in children. Obviously it is not only children that these poisonous non-foods affect but adults also. Every, so-called, dysfunctional family that exists consume poison on a grand scale. Recreational drugs, alcohol and smoking are just part of the picture, also included are artificial cereals, sweets, coffee, fizzy drinks, white bread, jams, margarine, crisps, and all other processed, artificial foods. Many people never, ever give their body anything fresh or natural, is it any wonder that they find it difficult to function properly? Many studies have shown that when criminals and delinquents clean up their diets then their behaviour improves enormously. I am certain that the cure for most, (but obviously not all), criminal behaviour is simply a healthy, natural diet which goes beyond a vegetarian or vegan diet and excludes any foods which no other animal would consume.

So, although diet is often seen totally independent of spiritual factors, it is an essential factor to consider if we want to attain higher levels of consciousness, since the body is the temple of the soul and has a profound effect upon it.

Another way of looking at this subject is to consider that eating is a way of interacting with the universe. Every interaction changes us in some way and the way it changes us depends on the quality of the interaction. If we engage in an unnatural interaction with little awareness (such as eating sweets) it will pull us down, whereas if we engage in a natural interaction with mindfulness (such as eating fresh fruit with appreciation) it will lift us up. Obviously the same is true of all our interactions not just with food - the way we interact with nature, people, animals and every other aspect of reality will effect our energy levels.

> *Love is the ultimate nutrient.*
> *NOLAN JOHN*

So, the link between the spiritual and the physical goes both ways: our attitude, our feelings, our levels of inner peace, etc, affect our level of physical health *and* vice versa. The foods we eat play an enormous part in how we feel in all of our day to day interactions with others. Sometimes you may feel very irritated with someone not because of their behaviour but because of what you had for breakfast!

If you want to develop along the spiritual path it is essential to clean up the temple of your soul. One of the most powerful ways to do this is to fast for extended periods exclusively on water. All the great spiritual teachers have put great emphasis on fasting as a path to enlightenment and many recommend long fasts of 4o days or more. This is obviously for the dedicated individual, but I believe that short fasts starting with just one day or a weekend can be extremely beneficial for everyone.

Transcending our Limitations

WHERE ARE "OUR" MEMORIES?

The blocks which are present within nearly every human being on this planet have repercussions on every one of our human qualities - physical, emotional, spiritual, and psychological. I think it is very important to consider the concept of memory in trying to get to understand more deeply what we are.

It is possible that memories aren't localised, i.e. they don't have any location, and therefore the question of this heading is a meaningless one. However, I believe that it is well worth considering. The reason that I put the word "our" in inverted commas, is because they might not be ours at all.

I would like to begin by considering the question of not just where is the source of our knowledge but what enables us to "tune in" to it and what blocks us from tuning in.

After we have learnt something and we then consider the information to be inside our memory we call tuning in remembering and when we can't tune in again we say we have forgotten. However, there is a very important distinction between "forgetting" and "not remembering". Forgetting implies that the memories have gone, never again to be accessed, whereas not remembering simply implies that the ability to recall the information is impaired even though the memories may still be "stored" somewhere. It is very useful to ask the question whether, according to these definitions, we ever really forget anything? The answer, surprisingly, is - probably not.

Just because you can't remember something,
does not mean that you have forgotten it!

When a part of the temporal cortex of the brain is artificially stimulated with an electric current, memories of past events can come flooding back as clearly as if they were being relived at that moment - with all the sights, sounds, smells, tastes and tactile sensations of the original event. Memories of long-forgotten experiences can come forth as if they were happening here and now. Participants of this neurological experiment often express surprise at the clarity of the memories of events in their past which they otherwise would never have been able to recall, (except perhaps under hypnosis). This neurological experiment suggests, but obviously does not prove, that we may never *really* forget anything, all that happens is that we lose the ability to recall.

So where, if anywhere, are these memories stored? Some say that electrical stimulation of the temporal cortex gives us evidence that memories are stored in the brain, however, other experiments have shown that there is no specific location for the storage of memories within the brain. One, cruel thirty year study involved teaching rats maze-running skills and then cutting out a part of their brain to test for memory loss. This study revealed that whatever part was cut out there was no loss in memory, only a loss in efficiency - this implies that the memories of the maze were not located in any particular part of the brain. Some scientists say that this doesn't prove that the memories are not stored in the brain, only that they are not localised - maybe a little is stored in every cell of the brain. I believe that any scientist who engages in such a disgusting activity as cutting out a part of the brain of a living rat must be so out of touch with nature that they are certainly unlikely to come to any conclusions which are in touch with nature. A mechanistic scientist must come to mechanistic conclusions whatever the results of the experiment.

Non-mechanistic scientists suggest that memories aren't stored in the brain at all, they are stored in a non-localised field which the brain tunes into by a process of resonance. Dr Rupert Sheldrake calls this "the morphogenetic field" - this is a type of information field that we are all immersed in, and can tune in to, by a process called morphic resonance.

What seems clear is that the temporal cortex is involved in the process of recall, but this does not mean that the memories are stored there. Even though we can't say where memories are stored, it is certainly true that we have access to an incredible amount of information - we just need to learn how to get access to it more easily.

It might be the case that we not only potentially have access to the memories of *everything* that we have ever read, learnt or done, every conversation that we have ever had, every flower that we have ever smelt, every food that we have ever tasted, and so on, but we might have potential access to all information. So, it might be that the information available to us - if we know how to get access to it, is infinite - not just immense but *infinite*. Carl Jung called this *the collective unconscious*, which contains all the knowledge gained by every human being that lives, has ever lived, *and will ever live*, on this planet.

If you notice I didn't include the term "collective unconscious" in table 1 on page 18, this would have been very difficult to include in any particular column - is it mind? is it western God? is it eastern God? The term collective unconscious encompasses all of these - it is an energy field which we are immersed in, a consciousness which we tap into, the source of memory, the creativity which artists tune into and the essence of what we are that we may access during meditation, deep relaxation or moments of inspiration.

There is a reading method rapidly becoming popular called *photo-reading,* this is very different to speed-reading. Photo-reading uses a scanning method which puts the information of a book directly into the subconscious without the conscious part of the mind being aware of it. The average "fast" reader, reads at speeds of about say 300 words per minute, a speed reader can attain speeds of 1000 to as much as 2000 words per minute. However, a photo reader can attain speeds of 20 000 words a minute, this is equivalent to at least 1 page per second. In other words, it is possible to "read" a book as fast as you can turn the pages. This sounds impossible by conventional standards but it is based on the principle that when you look at a page in a certain state of consciousness, there is a part of you that takes in *everything* and the tricky bit then is being able to access this information at will. The key is to trust. This is an equal part of the skill of photo-reading and involves developing a total trust for both the process of absorbing the information and the intuitive recall which is based on stating the first thing that comes into your mind. So, if someone photo reads a book and is then asked a question about the book, if they think long and hard about it they may not know the answer but if they say the first answer that comes into their mind after being asked, it is usually, in at least 80% of cases, the correct answer. Many experienced photo-readers after having read a whole book in a few minutes score 70 to 80 percent in comprehension tests. They may answer spontaneously and then think to themselves "where did that come from, I didn't know that I knew that?".

One possible explanation of this phenomenon is that *we all know everything already* and we don't actually need to read any books. If we know everything already then we can look at photoreading as a revision process where we are simply reminding ourselves of what we already know.

Photoreading a book may be a method of making a little less tenuous the link with that field of knowledge - "the collective unconscious". Maybe this is actually where all our insights come from. When you are having an inspirational conversation and realise something you didn't realise before, you may like to claim ownership of the insight and think "oh, aren't I clever to realise something so profound". The truth, however, is that you simply "tuned in" to the field of awareness which we all potentially have access to. If you can accept that we may be immersed in a field of infinite knowledge then the idea of photo-reading will not be too difficult to accept. The secret is really to learn to quieten the rational mind and trust more our incredible intuitive faculties, we will then move closer to that state of oneness which is often referred to as "Enlightenment".

WHAT IS ENLIGHTENMENT?

The ultimate goal of all spiritual endeavours is enlightenment. For me to attempt to explain what this is may be similar to a blind man trying to explain what light is. However, despite the difficulties and limitations resulting from my unenlightened state I will nevertheless attempt to convey my understanding of what enlightenment is both from information gained from wise masters throughout history, and from my own insights.

Enlightenment is often considered to mean a state where all truth is known, where there is a total understanding of everything. Obviously this has very little, if anything, to do with intellectual knowledge and understanding as we know it from our "normal" education. True understanding has more to do with being connected to universal consciousness. To put it simply I believe that enlightenment is the state where all the barriers have broken down which usually stop the realisation of our oneness with everything.

The only way to express the profundity of this incredible state of being is to attempt to describe some of the qualities of a perfectly enlightened man as described by masters of various religions through the ages. I have listed a few of these qualities below.

As you read through the qualities I have listed you may like to think of Jesus or Buddha or any other great master that you respect.

An enlightened person is a person who is calmed, has no anger, fear or pride and has eliminated all personal cravings.

An enlightened person has no longing for the future or sadness about the past, they live in the moment and accepts things as they are.

An enlightened person is unattached to all worldly possessions including their own body.

An enlightened person has extinguished the craving even to exist.

An enlightened person holds no bad feelings towards anyone.

An enlightened person is not arrogant, and makes no comparisons with the world as superior, inferior or equal.

An enlightened person feels that nothing belongs to him and also that nothing doesn't belong to him.

An enlightened person is free of greed and possessiveness.

An enlightened person does not hold any firm views.

An enlightened person has total control over all matter and energy.

An enlightened person experiences an unimaginable level of physical health.

YOU HAVE ALL THE ANSWERS

If you have a major problem in your life the first thing that you might want to do is to talk to someone about it. Depending on the nature of the problem you may want to speak to a good friend, a naturopath, a financial advisor, a priest, a counsellor, a teacher, a psychiatrist, a wise master, or anyone else who you believe might help you to gain a relevant insight towards the nature of your problem. Whether any of these people can help or not depends both on their level of wisdom, and on how much they are in harmony with life and with you.

> *If you can't find the truth right where you are,*
> *where else do you think you will find it?*
> THE BUDDHA

I believe that **every problem has a solution**, and if while suffering through a problem you could speak to the wisest person on earth the solution would become immediately apparent. You may say: "this doesn't help me, because I don't know the wisest person on earth!" The surprising truth is that you do - you are that person! You are potentially the wisest person on Earth. **The answer to almost any question you could ask is within you.**

> *Be afraid of nothing. You have within you:*
> *All wisdom, all power, all strength, all understanding.*
> EILEEN CADDY

You are the best person to ask if you keep getting headaches or are always miserable but don't know why, and *you* are the one who best knows what you really need in life and what is required to make you happy and healthy. The big question is: how do we ask and how do we listen? I will be dealing with this important question in due course.

We are all in this classroom called earth
trying to discover something - the ultimate,
and we are all looking for it externally. Where is it?
If we only turn our direction back upon ourselves,
we will discover, it's right here where I am.
LESTER LEVENSON

WHAT IS WISDOM?

Wisdom has nothing to do with memory and intellectual ability but has much more to do with love and compassion - it is a measure of true awareness and shows how much has been learned from living in harmony with life. Wisdom is the quality of understanding and compassion that comes when the soul is residing in a clean body, this is when we are in a loving, connected state.

A man's wisdom can be measured not by what he
knows nor what he says but by how he lives.
To live wisely means to live lovingly.

Just as love connects us to the source of wisdom, and enhances our creative abilities; judgmental, evil or unkind thoughts block us from it - so we must make every effort to avoid thoughts of this type.

Wisdom enters not into a malicious mind.
RABELAIS

Just as love is a state of being and not a feeling, it is also true to say that wisdom is a state of being and not a state of mind.

To gain wisdom, you first have to connect - to love - this is the main characteristic of any true philosopher. In fact, the word philosophy comes from the Greek words "Philos" (Φιλος) meaning friend or lover and "Sofia" (Σοφια) meaning wisdom. So, literally, the word philosophy means "friend of wisdom", and a philosopher is a "lover of wisdom".

> *Neither a lofty degree of intelligence nor imagination*
> *nor both together go to the making of a genius.*
> *Love, love, love, that is the soul of genius.*
> ARMADIUS MOZART

A criticism often made of philosophy is that there is no point posing a question which has no answer, that there is no point discussing something if you can't ever come to a conclusion. However, the point of philosophical debate is not to come to conclusions, since this is synonymous with coming to a full stop or a dead end. The aim of philosophical conversation is to stimulate ideas which help us to make connection with truth. Wisdom will only come if we can keep an open mind which means not holding firmly to any established beliefs or set doctrines - those who hold no *fixed* system of belief are more likely to attain wisdom than those who do, and so we do not want to "come to conclusions". However, if philosophy remains an intellectual activity, it is simply another academic subject, separated from, and irrelevant to everyday life.

Someone studying philosophy on an intellectual level can be compared to a person who reads book after book about swimming without ever going near the water.

> *Philosophy isn't something to learn,*
> *it's something to live.*

As I explained in the first section of the book, "truth" can't be known on an intellectual level, it is something to *experience*. The

106

purpose of philosophical debate is to increase our awareness so that we can move to higher energy states and thereby experience truth.

Creativity and talent are not innate qualities, they are a measure of how connected one is to the ultimate source of wisdom which permeates the universe. Creativity comes from removing the blocks that stop most of us from getting access to the immense source of knowledge and wisdom which is available to us all if we can only learn how to connect with it.

In biology the words *inspire* and *expire* are used to mean *breathed in* and *breathed out* respectively. If an insight seems to just come to us all of a sudden, then we speak of being inspired, as if we breathed in, or inspired, the wisdom from an external source. Most creative geniuses such as artists, poets, musicians, inventors and scientists, acknowledge the fact that they don't personally create their great works - they are created through them - it is as if they act as a channel or receiver tuning into something greater than themselves.

> *True creativity comes out of stillness.*
> DR. KATHERINE WATSON

An important way that we can make contact with this source of creative genius is by practising following our intuition. Creative people often have a highly developed intuitive ability. The more you practice following your intuition the clearer the messages get. But what is intuition? Let's analyse the word. The word *intuition* means *in*ner *tuition*, i.e. **intuition means to be taught from within.** Our intuition is our link to the wisdom within, this is literally our inner-tuition. The extent to which we are able to follow our intuition determines the quality of *every* decision that we make in life.

Without going out of my door I can know all things on Earth,
without looking out of my window I can know
the ways of heaven. For the further
one travels the less one knows.
LAO TZU.

WHAT IS BLOCKING US?

Let us now consider what causes the barriers that stop us from connecting to who we really are and therefore appreciating the immense beauty of life. Looking at the body wholistically, there are various factors that might create the blocks which stop us connecting to the beauty of life, the most important are:

1) A junk food diet and other poisons which may be voluntarily put into the body such as alcohol, recreational drugs, etc. These poisons alter our behaviour and distort all of our perceptions.

2) A negative self-image and low self-esteem which may make us feel unworthy and create self-abusive behaviour. I am not referring here only to drugs, alcohol, smoking, junk food, etc, but to all actions which sabotage ourselves.

3) A medical system which keeps the body in a poisoned state by using suppressive medication to stop the body healing itself of accumulated toxins. Most acute diseases are actually healing crises which the body sets up as a means of cleaning itself up. E.g. Vomiting, diarrhoea, skin rashes, fever, colds, etc. Suppressing these diseases is what causes the state of low level health - fatigue, lethargy, depression, irritability, weakness, etc.

4) Our western so-called "education" (which is really a mis-education). This builds layer upon layer of mechanistic doctrine which takes us away from our centre.

5) Our ego which lives by the principle "look after number one".

6) Blaming others for our unfortunate situation and holding on to negative emotions, particularly resentment, bitterness and hate.

It is important to realise the inner power that we have to change our life in any way that we desire, in other words we need to let go of the victim mentality. These negative emotions block the free flow of energy around the body which inhibits the detoxification process which cleans up the bloodstream and lightens the toxic burden.

The most efficient way to "enlighten" the body of its toxic burden is to hold love in your heart and the next most efficient way is to eat natural foods with love and appreciation.

Once we lighten ourselves of the toxic burden and become pure inside, our behaviour can be nothing but perfect. It will then become easier to love and therefore we will be on a virtuous circle towards ever increasing states of health, spirituality and well being.

There are two main ways that we can express "the cause of ill health" or "the cause of the blocks which create most of our limitations", these are:
• Poisons flowing through the bloodstream.
• An inhibition of the body's eliminatory mechanisms.

Many health food fanatics put all their emphasis on the diet and ignore the factors which enhance eliminatory efficiency. In other words they worry about the input while neglecting to consider the importance of the output. The body's eliminatory efficiency is determined primarily by how much we love - not only people but life in general, nature, and everything in the universe - both manifest and unmanifest.

There are infinite ways to discover your true being,
but love holds the brightest torch.

I know this from experience. I have met many health food fanatics whose food choices are determined by fear and worry and although they eat "good" foods, they are not themselves healthy. On the other hand, I have met others who eat with love and appreciation and although the foods aren't as pure the body extracts the best from them and eliminates the rest. However, this does not give us a licence to put any old rubbish in our body.

Although I believe that love is the main factor that determines our health and our level of enlightenment, this is something that most people find difficult to grasp as a practical step. It is easier to communicate to the average person about the importance of cleaning up the input stage. In other words to look carefully at the diet - but obviously without developing a worry or a fear regarding what we are eating.

Fear is the most damaging toxin;
Love is the most powerful nutrient.
NOLAN JOHN

The question of nutrition is very important to consider, since eating unnatural foods - as man does in enormous quantities - may be one of the main reasons why we have departed so much from our natural instincts and our connection to universal consciousness. Eating natural, raw foods may be *one of* the most important ways to connect us back to our true nature.

PRACTICAL STEPS TO ENLIGHTENMENT

Unless you try to do something beyond what you have already mastered you will never grow.
THOMAS ALLEN

Considering the above list of the 5 main causes of internal barriers, here are several practical steps that we can take to connect with our true essence:

1) Eat natural foods in their natural state - primarily green leaves, soaked hemp seeds, a variety of vegetables, fruits and sprouted seeds.

2) Practice silence and stillness - spend at least 15 minutes each day doing absolutely nothing, with as little as possible around to distract or entertain your senses. This is the most powerful way to tune into your inner voice. Don't *try* to relax or meditate, just let yourself be. If you want to make contact with your higher self or spiritual essence, this won't be achieved by concentrated effort but will just happen spontaneously if you allow yourself to be silent. You will be surprised what you can discover in the stillness. It's in our solitude that we can get to know ourselves best. Most people never learn to listen to their inner voice because they are too busy focusing on external distractions and entertainments.

You don't have to do anything to find the self, you have to stop doing anything.
DR. DEEPAK CHOPRA

3) Meditation - in a way this can be seen as an extension of the silence practice just mentioned, but here you are using a specific method such as repeating a mantra, or

watching your breath, or any one of the meditation techniques which I shall explain in the next section.

4) Live life as a meditation - that is practice being fully focused in the moment putting full attention to whatever you are doing or feeling.

5) While relaxing, try repeating to yourself suggestions such as:

- I have all knowledge and wisdom within me.
- I am connected to the higher consciousness within me.
- All solutions come to me easily and effortlessly.

6) Get out into the sunshine, breathe in the fresh air, engage in natural exercise such as walking, gardening, swimming, etc.

7) Practice the appreciation of beauty - it is the experience of the appreciation of beauty that connects you to the object of beauty and therefore moves you into the state of love. To spend a little time each day appreciating the beauty within nature and people is actually a practice in cultivating love.

8) Be open to those thoughts that just spontaneously come to you in idle moments while you are sitting in silent relaxation, doing nothing, meditating or just day-dreaming.

9) Keep a journal or notebook, write down as a heading, the question that you require to be answered, and then just write down whatever comes into your mind regarding the question. If you do this regularly, you will be surprised at what comes out - you will sometimes write down profound truths that you didn't even realise you knew!

10) You can follow a similar process in conversation with

close friends as with your journal. If you are willing to be totally open with someone and you can listen to each other non-judgmental, you will be surprised at the pearls of wisdom that you both begin to express.

11) Be open to the advice or information given to you during your interactions with others and take notice of life's events which seem to be telling you something and pointing you in a certain direction.

12) Develop an easy-going carefree attitude to life. Nothing matters. Laugh at life. A sense of humour takes away the seriousness from life and makes everything lighter. Make it your intention to have a good laugh every day.

13) Study your dreams. All ancient cultures have put considerable importance on the value of our dreams. Your dreams are another facet of your life and the more you can pay attention to their content, the greater will be your connection with this other dimension of reality.

The shamans see dreams as an entry into another dimension which is just as real, if not more real, than this dimension which we think of as "reality".

Once Chuang Chou dreamt he was a butterfly;
a butterfly flitting and fluttering about, happy with himself
and doing as he pleased. He didn't know he was Chuang Chou.
Suddenly he woke up and there he was, solid and
unmistakable Chuang Chou. But now he didn't
know if he was Chuang Chou who had
dreamt he was a butterfly,
or a butterfly dreaming
he was Chuang Chou.
ZHUANG ZHOU

THE POWER OF MEDITATION

People who practice meditation begin to discover
a deeper aspect of life and an ease, a joy,
a happiness which is not dependent
upon outer circumstances.

F. W. WHITING

If the claims are to be believed, there is almost no area of our lives which the practice of meditation won't improve. Meditation is often considered to be a spiritual practice, however it can be of benefit to us on all levels of our being - not only on the spiritual, but also on the physical, psychological and emotional levels.

Some of the claimed benefits of meditation include: Slowing down the ageing process, improving motor co-ordination, strengthening the immune system, preventing hypertension, curing headaches, stopping ulcers, reducing the risk of cancer and heart disease, improving memory and concentration, enhancing our ability to deal with stress, increasing self-confidence and self-esteem, enhancing emotional stability, increasing energy and vitality, helping sound sleep, reducing anxiety, creating a greater sense of inner peace,..... and the list goes on.

Man is ill
because he is never still.

PARACELSUS

There is now scientific proof that meditation does have beneficial effects on our health on many levels - this is no longer an unsubstantiated claim. Scientific studies carried out on large groups of meditators show that their physiological organs function with an efficiency which is equivalent to someone several years younger than their chronological age.

114

The wonderful thing about meditation is that you can practice it, irrespective of your religious beliefs. It can be of great value whether you are an Atheist, Agnostic, Hindu, Jew, Christian, Buddhist, Muslim, or whatever.

Meditation is very misunderstood in the west. Many people take it to mean sitting down cross-legged and totally clearing your mind - this might be what some people do when they meditate, but there are many forms of meditation and the word generally has a much wider meaning than this.

The sitting position is not at all relevant to the practice of meditation, as in any form of deep relaxation the important thing is that you are comfortable. However, if you are sitting and feelings of discomfort arise, sometimes it can be a very useful practice to just stay with it - simply "watch" the discomfort rather than immediately adjust in order to avoid it.

While meditating, it is not always essential that you are sitting - there are some forms of meditation that you can do as you walk. This practice involves being fully focused in the moment, putting full attention on to each step or on to the details of walking rather than allowing your mind to drift wherever it wants.

You can, of course, meditate while lying down, however, it is not always a good idea to meditate in this way since it may cause you to fall asleep.

There are two main schools of thought on the purpose of meditation:
* To tame the mind so that it is not the master of your soul but you are its master.
* To quieten the mind and thereby make contact with the essence of your being.

Nowhere can man find a calmer or more
untroubled haven than in his own soul.
MARCUS AURELIUS

As you may realise these are two ways of expressing the same thing since once the mind is tamed and you have control of it, you can then get into a state where you are in touch with your essence. The difference between these two schools of thought become clearer when we express each in terms of what to do when you meditate. Is the aim to control the mind by directing it on to a specific thought or image, or is it to silence the mind - to stop thinking and thereby make contact with the soul? Well I believe that the ultimate goal is the latter, however to empty the mind is nearly an impossible feat for the average human being, especially for the typical city dweller with such a constant stream of distractions both while we are keeping busy and while we are resting. Most westerners while resting want to continue to be distracted and so they turn on the T.V., radio, music system, or go to a place where they can be "entertained".

Most of the evils in life
arise from man's being unable to sit still in a room.
BLAISE PASCAL

While you are successfully meditating, the body may become as relaxed as when you are in a deep sleep, the main difference being that during meditation you are fully conscious.

To have an *empty* mind may be something which may happen spontaneously, but for most people, it is not something that happens due to making a conscious effort. So, what we need to do first is direct the mind on to a particular idea, meditation generally involves focusing the mind on one specific thing. The intention is that your mind is "one-pointed" - totally focused and not wandering about all the time.

The most common types of meditation are:

1. MANTRA MEDITATION - Meditate on a meaningless word, such as "reema", "vraam", "rah" or whatever - you can make up your own if you wish or you can choose one from eastern teachings, such as "OM". Repeat the word internally, over and over again, effortlessly put your attention only on the sound of the word. If your mind begins to wander then gently bring it back on to the mantra. There are some who say that your mantra must be chosen for you by a wise master (who charges a lot of money for this service), but I believe that this is totally unnecessary - you are the best person to decide what sound is right for you.

2. SUGGESTIVE MEDITATION - Meditate on a word or small phrase, such as "Tranquillity", "Love", "Unity" or "I am at peace".

3. MEDITATION ON THE BREATH - As you breathe as naturally as possible simply "watch" the breath.

4. MUSIC MEDITATION - While sitting or lying comfortably with your eyes closed, listen to some relaxing music with full attention, feel yourself immersed in the beautiful sounds.

5. EXTERNAL IMAGE MEDITATION - Put full attention on to an external object such as a flower, a piece of fruit, a candle flame or a glass of water.

6. INTERNAL IMAGE MEDITATION - Meditate on a simple internal image such as a flower or a light.

7. LOVE MEDITATION - This is an extension of the appreciation of beauty exercise described in the last section. Hold a wonderful feeling for a particular person, animal, flower or landscape. Only think about the beauty within them, while putting attention to the good feeling within your heart.

8. LIFE MEDITATION - In some ways this is the most important one - be fully focused in everything you do in the day to day events of life. Give yourself fully to the task in hand, while making every effort to avoid thinking about what you have to do in five minutes from now.

The most important aspect of all these meditation techniques is to gain control of the mind so that as soon as it begins to wander you gently but firmly bring it back on to the thought, feeling or image that you have decided to focus upon. The ultimate goal is to gain such control that it ceases its endless activity and becomes calmed.

If you have never practised meditation but want to take it up, the first step is to become aware how the mind wants to be continually distracted or entertained.

Apart from practising any of the above forms of meditation you could try the following: When you rest make it your aim to do *nothing* - not even meditate. Try watching the television for an hour or two.... with it switched off. If you do this you may notice how much more aware you become of your body - you will become more "tuned in" to what is really important. You may also start to think something like "I can't just sit here doing nothing, it feels like a waste of time". This is a clear example of the mind trying to sabotage your attempts to get in touch with your soul. The mind is like a naughty monkey - constantly on the go and always wanting to be the master and sabotage your efforts to tame it. The truth is that it is far less of a waste of time to sit in front of the T.V. with it switched off than it would be to watch a very entertaining programme. Television, as well as other powerful forms of distraction, may be disconnecting us from our essence.

*We are relying on television as a
substitute for telepathy or direct connection
with universal consciousness.*
LISA CENERI

We are usually so busy *doing* things due to the continual distraction from all our activities that we lose touch with our *being*. One of the important benefits of meditation is that we learn *to be* not *to do*. Remember, we are human beings not human doings.

*....the mind of man so caught in external
pursuits and inner conflicts needs a technique of letting go,
a technique of not doing.*
F. W. WHITING

Regular practice of meditation leads to a profound sense of inner peace and the ultimate aim of meditation is said to be to make contact with the deepest essence of our being, to know who we really are and experience our connection with nature. Once we achieve this state of being, life takes on a totally new and richer meaning.

KEEP OPEN TO LIFE

*There is none so blind as he who will not see,
we must not close our minds,
we must let our thoughts be free.*
RAY STEVENS
(EVERYTHING IS BEAUTIFUL)

There are many ways to get more in touch with the spiritual part of ourselves - through being open to life, peaceful relaxation, prayer, positive suggestions, meditation, appreciating life and nature, feeling love, helping people, eating natural foods, and so on. Apart from cultivating love, openness is probably the most important quality necessary for us to find wisdom, develop a trust in life and become in harmony with ourselves.

> *With an open mind, you will be open-hearted.*
> *Being open-hearted, you will act royally.*
> *Being royal, you will attain the divine.*
> LAO TZU

To be open is absolutely essential for our development - to be open to new ideas, to be open to different ways of thinking, to be open to see things in new ways, and to be open to express what we truly feel. We must try to keep our minds open by looking, listening and above all doubting what we already know. Just as we must keep our hearts open by loving and trusting in life, we must also keep our minds open not by attaching to what we already know, but by allowing new, creative ideas to flow.

> *An open mind allows ideas to flow.*
> *An open heart allows love to flow.*

Just as clinging onto people creates unhealthy relationships, clinging onto ideas is also unhealthy, since, once we feel that we know something for sure we close our minds to other possibilities. As soon as we hear someone say: "I strongly believe that ...." we can be sure that this person won't have an open mind that will enable him to listen to other points of view. The most damaging consequences of closed mindedness is intellectual ignorance. Attachment to fixed viewpoints leads to ignorance, since the mind is, in this situation, unable to take on board new ideas. The state of *ignorance* is created by *ignoring* information which is fully available to someone if they will only look and listen.

The highest form of ignorance is
to reject something you know nothing about.
DR. WAYNE W. DYER

For life to be our teacher we must be open to the lessons that life provides. It is very important for us to open our minds to different ways of looking at life while questioning everything that we are told. We must be willing to let go of the old so that we can take in the new and develop in a healthy way. If someone feels that they already have all the answers they will not set off on the voyage of discovery that is required to attain the state of wisdom.

How could we ever discover new territory
if we were not lost in the first place?
ANDREA PHOTIOU

To discover new territory we must not only be lost, but we must also be aware that we are lost. With this realisation comes the humbleness and openness that leads us on our quest for truth.

If you shut your door to all errors,
truth will be shut out.
RABINDRANATH TAGORE

It is essential, not to confuse "developing an independence of mind" with "thinking you are always right", the former is based on open-mindedness whereas the latter is based on closed-mindedness. There is, similarly, an enormous difference between "doubting what you hear" and "closing your mind due to assuming it is wrong anyway".

Strive to be self-confident with humbleness,
and doubting with openness.

Some people confuse open-mindedness with gullibility because an open minded person is always willing to listen to new ideas. However, gullibility is the quality of accepting an idea without appropriate evaluation - many closed minded people have come to attach to their ideas in this way. They may have come to their opinion by hearing it many times and taken it on board without any independent thought or analysis.

> *The highest form of ignorance is*
> *to **accept** something you know nothing about.*
> NOLAN JOHN

Recently I had an enjoyable discussion with a Jehovah's Witness who said "I know that anyone who belongs to a religion thinks that their religion is right, but my religion *really is* right". Although this may sound amusing to any external observer, who doesn't belong to this particular religion, it is a very, very common attitude indeed, not only in religion but in many systems of thought. Most people believe that their way *really is the way*. A few years ago while I was practising a certain form of Kung Fu I was chatting with one of the black belts and he said "Most martial artist think that their style is the best, but I can assure you that this is the best style you can find". This is the attitude which blocks the flow of knowledge and insight and hence the chance of gaining wisdom.

> *Watch that in your quest for truth,*
> *yourself you don't deceive,*
> *for the answer lies not only in your eyes,*
> *but in what others, too, believe.*
> ANDREA PHOTIOU

Some may argue that before they came to the views that they now hold strongly, they were initially open-minded, considered all possible viewpoints, and then came to a clear conclusion and formed a strong belief, which was based on evidence. Well, the fact is that, despite the fact that the view came to them while they were open-minded, once they decided to hold strongly to it, their mind could no longer remain open. This is why many people, tend, as they get older, to form fixed views and slowly close off their minds to new ideas, whereas, the young are generally more open and receptive. We must try to maintain this receptivity as we get older, for if we are closed-minded and closed-hearted we will evolve at a much slower rate.

Look at ideas
without emotional investment.
NOLAN JOHN

There is nothing worse than a religion that teaches "you must beware of being open for fear of corruption". Many religions and cults teach their followers this and it is a clever way to maintain obedient followers.

It is ironic that all those Sunday mornings while the congregation sit in church hearing statements such as "be careful of evil cults that can corrupt your mind", "beware of hypnotists - they try to control your mind", "keep away from clairvoyants - they are devil workers", etc, they are actually allowing their minds to be controlled and subjecting themselves to the very evil dangers that they are being warned against. **It is often the religion itself that is dangerous and not the open-minded belief system that it warns against.**

We are conscious beings and as we live, our consciousness is evolving by taking in energy in two ways:

1) In the form of information if we are open-minded.
2) In the form of love if we are open-hearted.

123

From this we can see that to evolve we need to be open, we need to connect, we need to love, we need to seek the truth - in this way we will allow energy to come into us from the universe, which makes us more energetic, more conscious and more loving beings.

Some people go through life totally disconnected, with a closed mind and a closed heart and then they wonder why they feel so empty and are not making progress. It is very easy to become trapped by one's own mind-set, and there is nothing more liberating than letting go of long held beliefs which aren't serving us.

> *You don't know you've been entrapped*
> *until you have been set free.*
> EARL NIGHTINGALE

Some people rely on science to "prove" that their view is the correct one and that they are therefore justified to hold to it with conviction. However, as I have explained science is based on a mechanistic, deterministic world view whose foundations are laid by a set of assumptions all of which are very open to question.

> *The new "truths" of science are continually replaced by*
> *newer "truths". Viewed as a whole, therefore, science proceeds*
> *only from one error to another and the wise man will put no*
> *more reliance on the very latest scientific theory*
> *than he did on the one which it replaced.*
> THOMAS ALLEN

It is certainly a mistake to think that a currently accepted view is any more valid than a viewpoint which was accepted in "more primitive times".

*Neither modernity nor antiquity is a
measure of an ideas validity.*
ANONYMOUS

We would be well advised to try to hold onto our beliefs like we
might hold a butterfly, with an almost open hand as opposed to a
tight grip that would kill it. It is easy to see the result in others
when they hold on tightly to what they believe, you can't get
through to them, and if you try, it's like knocking your head
against a brick wall. If you do feel like this it is important to ask
yourself the question "why am I trying to force my point of view
on to them anyway?" Everyone would feel much more
comfortable if we could all hold our views loosely, like we might
hold a butterfly

You cannot shake hands with a clenched fist.
INDIRA GHANDI

THE POWER OF CONSCIOUSNESS

Some of the ideas of this section may be considered by some to
be a bit too far-fetched and may require a fresh, open-minded
outlook to contemplate. It does seem that when we delve into the
nature of the universe, we discover that the truth about reality is
extremely, weird, bizarre, peculiar, strange and above all
paradoxical.

A paradox is something that is both true and not true at the same
time. How can this be? Well, our intellect says "it can't be!
Something is either true or it's not true, but it can't be both."
However this is a statement about the intellect not about the
universe. The universe itself is paradoxical. Here are a few
examples, but be warned: don't try too hard to analyse them for
they might drive you crazy!

* Nothing is permanent, but everything is eternal.
* All there is, is "now, but the present doesn't exist.
* The future is the past.
* The universe is finite but has no boundary (maybe!)
* Matter is both a particle and a wave.
* Humans are actually a part of universal consciousness but we are also all of it at the same time

Don't worry if these statements don't mean anything to you. They are not simply playing with words, I am trying to introduce the idea that the universe may be stranger than we realise and that we can't intellectually analyse everything (even if it might be fun trying!). However, when we do intellectually analyse certain deep concepts such as *what I am* and *what the universe is*, we may develop insights which help our consciousness develop or help us to get more in touch with our essence. So, here goes:

As I explained before, what *you* are, is the observer of everything that you experience. All that you observe - tables, chairs, rocks, mountains, stars, your own body, and even your thoughts and feelings are all part of the scenery and not part of the observer. However, the scenery is created by the observer as I shall attempt to explain.

The observer - which is pure consciousness - is permeating the whole universe and, here is the first bit which you may find a little hard to accept at first - **the act of observation creates the object under observation.** Wow, this is a deep one, it implies that if there was no observation there would be nothing to observe. Consciousness itself is creating the manifest universe.

When I was a small child I began asking the question *Why does the universe exist?* And then I got to thinking *What if it didn't? What if there was no universe? What if there was nothing?* To me this has always been, and still is, the most mind blowing concept there is - what is nothing? Try to imagine for a moment, not "nothing in the universe" but *no universe.* This is an impossible concept to imagine, because something (your imagination) can't imagine nothing, only nothing (?) can imagine nothing - this is a play with words but I will continue to play a little more since this can be very useful to creating insights. It seems that no thing in the universe is nothing and that everything is something, but does this mean that nothing does not exist or does it mean that no thing exists?

Some scientists have proposed the idea that **the universe is a quantum fluctuation of nothing.** But what causes "the nothing" to undergo a quantum fluctuation? (Don't worry if you don't understand the question!).

> *All around I see nothing pretending to be something,*
> *emptiness pretending to be fullness.*
> CONFUCIOUS

Is your mind going haywire at the moment? Don't worry if it is, since that's the point. Even though the intellect can't understand these concepts, this doesn't mean that they are meaningless gobbledygook! Even though I can't explain clearly what I want to say in words, it is still possible that you might resonate with the concepts that are beyond the words.

I find it interesting that the number zero has no value and yet it is the most powerful of all numbers, and mathematics, as we know it, couldn't exist without it.

> *Zero is the eternally existing nothing-ness*
> *that contains within it the potentiality of everything.*
> KENNETH MEADOWS

I have had many stimulating conversations with the scientist David A. Chalmers, whose ideas are encapsulated in the title of his stimulating book:

Everything is nothing.
DAVID A. CHALMERS

David explains, from a physicists point of view, how the manifest universe comes in to being by the "considerations" of consciousness. He prefers not to use the word "believe", because it tends to be psychologically and emotionally loaded, so instead he uses the word "consider". Whatever we *consider* to be true exists because of our consideration.

We don't have energy,
we create energy by the process of consideration.
DAVID A. CHALMERS

So, your whole reality is created by the process of consideration. **Your personal power is only limited by your ability to consider.** In a similar way, the state of the world is created by everyone's ability to consider.

FATE can be an acronym for
"from all thoughts everywhere".
In other words, the consciousness of the planet.
NEALE DONALD WALSCH

The reality that we observe on a global level is being created by the collective consciousness and the belief systems of everybody. We create our reality not only on an individual level but also on a global scale.

External reality is the sum total of all the considerations made by everybody.
DAVID A. CHALMERS

To reinforce this point, let's now return to the concept that the act of observation creates the object under observation. This is another way of saying that the manifest universe arises out of consciousness, this sounds very abstract and confusing so let me state it in this way: **All there is in the universe is observation.** I will now attempt to explain this statement in the following way:

When you taste an orange can you say where the taste is? Many people when asked this question say: "It's in the orange of course!", others may answer "It's in your tongue and your consciousness registers it", and others would answer "It's in the brain!". Well, maybe all of these answers are wrong. I am proposing the idea that **the taste of an orange only comes into existence when your tongue and the orange are interacting.** In other words, the act of observation brings the taste into being. Obviously, I am using the word "observation" here to mean *perceived by the observer, not just in a visual sense but in every sense.*

The way that we use our language we would always say that an orange has a certain taste, but strictly speaking the phrase "taste of an orange" only has a meaning when the orange is interacting with a living creature who is eating it, i.e. when it is being observed. This is true of all the qualities of an orange, not only its taste but also its smell, its texture, its colour, its shape, etc. These qualities are not within the orange, nor are they within the brain - all these qualities of an orange are generated by **the interaction of the orange with an observer.** Let me emphasise this with reference to the appearance of an orange: **The appearance of an orange is generated by *the interaction* of the orange with an observer.** Just as an orange has no intrinsic

129

taste it also has no intrinsic appearance! You may now want to say to this: "No, even if nobody is looking at an orange, it is still round!" but this isn't really the case as I will now explain:

Imagine an orange on its own in the universe, totally isolated and not interacting with anything. This is not actually possible because everything is interacting with everything else. But just suppose for one moment that the orange could be isolated, does it now have any meaning to speak about the taste of this orange? I would answer: "definitely not!" If you would answer yes, it is because your lifetime experiences of eating oranges has deeply conditioned you into believing that "*they* have a taste". Think about this point before reading on.

If it is meaningless to talk about the taste of an isolated orange, then it is similarly meaningless to talk about any of its other qualities. An isolated orange has no taste, no smell, no texture, no appearance, in fact *it has no qualities at all* - this is the same as saying that it doesn't exist. You may argue "But of course it has an appearance, *I can picture it,* all alone, just sitting there at the boundaries of the universe." The important thing to realise again is that your mental image is due to a life-time of experience of looking at oranges - visually interacting with them.

You may recognise within all this the age-old philosophical question "Would a fruit falling in the desert *on its own* make any sound? I'm sure that many a scientist has answered this by saying "Yes, it makes a sound since sound is just air in vibration and the air around the object would be set in to vibration by its fall, but no-one is around to hear the sound that it makes." I used to answer the question something like that, but now I believe that this is an invalid answer because sound is not simply vibrating air, it is a quality just like appearance, or taste - a quality set up by the interaction of observer and observed. **Sound is not simply the vibration of air molecules but the experience**

created when a vibrating object interacts with the consciousness of an observer via a vibrating eardrum.

I now want to go back to a point that I made earlier, and that is: An isolated orange *has no qualities at all* - this is the same as saying that it doesn't exist. When I say that it has no qualities this is saying much more than "the qualities cannot be described" or "that we cannot perceive them" If we can actually say that it has *no qualities* then it cannot exist since even empty space has some qualities, in other words an isolated orange is even more nothing than a perfect vacuum.

In a scientific sense the conclusion that can be drawn from this is that "nothing can be isolated", or should I say "no thing can be isolated" since "nothing" (if it exists), can't be isolated. Oh dear, I'm sorry if this is getting complicated, what I really want to say is **everything must be interacting with everything else**.

Now since something which isn't being observed by consciousness doesn't exist and then the act of observation creates its qualities, we can say that **the act of observation creates something from nothing.** However, I myself to some extent, can pull apart the sentence that I have just written, since according to the non-mechanistic, spiritual world view the statement "something which isn't being observed by consciousness" is invalid, since consciousness isn't something which belongs to individuals, it is something which permeates the entire universe. Therefore, **there is no thing in the universe which is not being observed by consciousness.**

In the beginning.....All That Is is all there was,
and there was nothing else. And so, All That Is.....was not.
For in the absence of something else, All That Is, is not
NEALE DONALD WALSCH

131

The qualities of everything manifest in the universe exist only because consciousness exists. Every thing and everything is made of consciousness or in other words no things could exist if there was no consciousness. Consciousness is what brings the manifest universe into being.

*The manifest universe
arises from consciousness.*

At this point I would like to reinforce a point which I made in the section *challenging the mechanistic world view,* and that is - the mechanistic paradigm propounds that the invisible (thought, mind, consciousness, fields, etc) arises from the visible (matter), whereas the spiritual world view as expounded above sees the opposite to be the case.

Consciousness sustains everything.

If we consider for a moment that as individuals, what we observe and the way we observe is determined to a large extent by our belief systems, then all of the above considerations take to a new level some of those statements which I included in my book - *You are what you think:*

Imagination precedes manifestation.
Your limitations are created by your beliefs.
Whatever you truly believe, you can manifest in your life.
The universe responds to your beliefs and expectations.
What you believe and expect becomes your reality.

All of these statements illustrate that we are incredibly powerful beings, but what is the new level to which these statements have been taken? Is there more meaning in them than simply that *we can do whatever we have the confidence to do?* Yes, they are saying far more than this. Whatever, enters human consciousness, begins in some way to exist in the universe - because the universe is made of/by human consciousness. Again, I apologise about the limitation of words - I said *human* consciousness, but it might convey a slightly more accurate meaning if I simply said consciousness, or maybe, universal consciousness, or even the light of consciousness. If all there is, is consciousness, then these are all the same, but the differences are created by what that consciousness is conscious of. Please forgive me if this appears to be meaningless waffle, I am expressing it in the best way I can but words are severely limiting here.

So, the reason that you can bring into manifestation whatever you hold in your consciousness, is not only because your actions are consistent with your beliefs, there is something deeper going on at the same time. Your beliefs affect your thoughts, your thoughts influence your consciousness and your consciousness in turn imprints itself on the universal cosmic template and begins to bring into existence whatever you are conscious of.

If our beliefs can actually influence the universe itself, it brings into question the whole concept of truth. Is there a reality out there independent of us, or are we co-creators of the reality that we observe? As you may guess I believe that the latter is closer to the way things actually are. This means that if two people have a whole set of beliefs which are in conflict with each other, it is possible that they may both be right. Our beliefs really do create our reality. In fact to go further - our beliefs help to create the universe. This means that it is possible to converse with someone with a totally different mindset to your own and state honestly: "You are totally right but I completely disagree with you". Each of us has our own reality - maybe there is no absolute truth after all!

BELIEVE IN MIRACLES
AND MAGIC

As a human race, we are held back both individually and collectively by the limitations that we have in our ability to consider.

If we could believe anything without limitations,
then we could achieve anything without limitations.

These limitations are like walls that are only broken down by awareness, rather than knowledge. It seems that intellectual knowledge simply builds the walls higher. Wisdom is often confused with the accumulation of knowledge or data, but this is not only wrong, it is the opposite to what is actually the case as I shall now explain.

I like to use the analogy of an onion where wisdom radiates from the centre. As small children, we were a very small onion with few layers - in touch with our centre, but as we "learned" and received our "wonderful education" the layers were built up, one after the other, until we had an enormous onion - very knowledgeable, very intelligent, but separated from the self, far from the centre - not very wise at all!

Both conventional education and social conditioning
cause children to lose their natural spontaneity,
and be separated from their being.

Young children have a natural curiosity, they really want to learn - not for "getting on in life" but for the sheer pleasure of knowing. This natural curiosity is usually thwarted by the conventional educational system of the western world, but we are all born with it. However, once the onion becomes a certain size when the layers created by years of indoctrination, mis-education and social brain-washing reach their maximum then the return journey must begin. Only after we shed all the layers can we find our centre and make connection with it.

*There is nothing more important in life
than our connection with nature.*

To improve our ability to consider and release our limitations, we need to peel off the layers created by self-limiting beliefs and the effects of a spiritually dampening mis-education. When you actually do peel off all the layers from the "onion" and get to the centre, what you find is something which permeates the whole universe; you will then better be able to appreciate and evaluate all the peeled off bits.

It takes a whole lifetime to learn nothing!
NOLAN JOHN

When you were a child, did you ever get a special feeling when you heard the rain beating on the window pain or the wind blowing through the trees? Did you ever get a wonderful feeling at Christmas time? Did you ever feel a kind of magical feeling when you walked through a natural environment such as a forest or wood? Were you ever aware of the presence of so-called mythical beings such as fairies, angels, elves, unicorns, or other magical creatures? Did you ever believe in magic? All of these experiences, represent being in touch with the centre, it seems to be an almost natural consequence of growing-up in our western culture to lose this very natural way of being.

When children express their "fantasies" or magical experiences to adults they may be told something like: "Don't be silly, fairies don't *really* exist", or "there is no such thing as magic." However, it is important to consider the possibility that children may be in touch with something magical or maybe spiritual (in some ways these are synonymous), rather than deluding themselves with totally self-created fantasies. It is just possible that the children may be correct in some of their perceptions and the adults may be wrong, and that by spending 12 years in an indoctrination centre called "School" our contact with our true essence is lost. Due to this spiritually damaging education, adults usually lose that special sense that children still have. If we use our "common sense", then the logical conclusion is that magic *must* exist since nothing can occur in anyone's fantasy more magical than life itself?

If you look back to the section *What is Enlightenment* and note the quality of an enlightened being: **An enlightened person has total control over all matter and energy.** This means literally that an enlightened person is a magician in the truest sense of the word.

Finding our centre, is all about becoming more aware, more connected to life, more loving, more spontaneous, more able to live in the moment and more in touch with nature. These are the qualities of both the wise man and the child.

The most important technique to help us get back to our centre is meditation, this is the tool that we can use at certain moments of the day, but it is what we do most of the day that matters. The rest of the time while we are not meditating, we could practice:

- Being fully aware in every situation.
- Loving ourselves, others, and all of life.
- Looking for what can be learned from every experience
- Living in the moment.
- Being spontaneous - like a child.
- Finding humour in many situations.
- Filling our imagination only with good images.
- Never giving consideration to thoughts of disaster.

Your perception of ultimate reality
is more limited than you thought,
and truth is more unlimited than you can imagine.
NEALE DONALD WALSCH

WE ARE UNLIMITED BEINGS

The ancients have declared since time immemorial the unlimited
potential which lies within each and every one of us,
but is buried under concepts of limitation.
LESTER LEVENSON

What I would like to explain in this section may at times sound very negative, but it is said with the intention to wake the reader up to the most empowering conclusion that we can come to and that is that we are beings of *infinite* potential.

To say we are "unlimited beings"
is not only saying that we are beings of great potential,
*it is saying that we are beings of **infinite** potential.*

If this is true, why are most of humanity so limited? Why do people feel like powerless victims with no control over their lives? The sad and apparently negative answer is **because that's how *they* want us to be.** And who are they? "They" are the unseen controllers of this planet. This planet is being controlled and manipulated by a small group who have incredible intellect and knowledge but who are very separated from their loving nature. The politicians who many think are controlling things on our behalf are actually doing all they can to keep the masses subservient and obedient in order to maintain the status quo.

Most people believe what they are conditioned to believe and have a very blinkered view of reality. In fact I believe that mainstream science (which I taught for several years) is just as much an indoctrinated dogma as is institutionalised religion. Mechanistic science is based on a set of assumptions that need to be constantly questioned and reassessed rather than held on to as fundamental and eternal truths. These assumptions form the foundations upon which the whole scientific paradigm is built. A few examples of assumptions which are accepted as fact are:

- The law of cause and effect - I believe that this isn't a "law" since spontaneous events are happening all the time.
- The concept of objectivity - I believe that there is no such thing as an objective observer since all things in the universe are interconnected and therefore everything influences everything else.
- The law of conservation of mass and energy - believe it or not this is not a law at all but an assumption which is made to be true. Physicists are introducing "fudge factors" all the time so that it can remain a law.

I could write a book on each of the above 3 points but for the purposes of this section the point I would like to make is that we mustn't cling on to a certain mindset as if it is fact. We must also avoid putting "science" on a pedestal and hold it up to be the path to truth - it is anything but. As I explained in the section *challenging the mechanistic world view,* the fundamental error of mainstream science is that it neglects consciousness as a fundamental property of the universe.

Two qualities inherent in consciousness
are attention and intention.
Attention energises and intention transforms.
DR. DEEPAK CHOPRA

The human race is indoctrinated not only through the media of T.V., newspapers, magazines, etc, but also through mainstream education which is actually an indoctrination designed to keep humanity from waking up to their true potential. I often call it mainstream *mis*-education, and I should know, I was highly mis-educated and it has taken me a few years to transcend all the nonsense which I was taught at college and university. In fact a fairly strong part of me always doubted what I was told and I often felt "there is definitely something missing here".

What lies behind us and what lies before us,
are tiny matters compared to what lies within us.
RALPH WALDO EMERSON

This is happening for a reason - the planetary controllers want to keep humanity in ignorance of their true potential because if people were to wake up to who and what they really are, they wouldn't be able to be controlled in the way that they presently are. So the various media put out information which will keep the masses subservient and easily controlled. The means by which they control is called *covert* control, because it is done in a very subtle and clever way so that those who are being controlled have no awareness that they are - in this way there will be no rebellion.

David Icke is one of the most awake authors who I have ever come across, if you would like to read more about how the human race is being manipulated read his books *And the truth shall set you free; I am me I am free* and *The biggest secret*.

Those who control the planet are in charge of all the big multi-national industries: the agricultural industry, the petrochemical industry, the arms industry, and especially the pharmaceutical and medical industries. Via these industries mankind is kept in a slightly (or in some cases very) poisoned state which keeps the body from functioning at its optimum. When the temple of your soul is in an unhealthy toxic state the soul itself cannot shine through as it would if it were housed in a pure, clean body. I actually believe that ageing is caused not by years but by the accumulation of poisons which cause blockages at both the physical and the etheric levels.

> *Ageing is caused not by time,*
> *but by the effects that occur in time.*

If you can stop this poisoning occurring you can halt the ageing process. This is one example of our incredible potential - **the ageing process is potentially avoidable.** When your body is clean at all levels and you are living in harmony with the purpose you were born for, then *you will not age.*

> *Life is a process of constant transformation, not decline,*
> *and therefore is full of potential for unlimited growth.*
> DR DEEPAK CHOPRA

You may find this hard to accept because of the deep conditioning that we have all had coming at us from a very young age from all sides that "everyone has to grow old", but as you are now aware I consider it essential to challenge every belief that we as human beings hold. I even challenge the belief (dogma?) that "death is inevitable".

> *Only those who will risk going too far*
> *can possibly find out how far one can go.*
> T. S. ELLIOT

I believe that every human being is potentially immortal - not only on a spiritual level (this goes without saying) but also on a physical level as well. **Physical immortality is a possibility.**

140

You have no limits
except those you hold onto in your mind.
When you let go of these limits,
you can have, do, or be, whatever you desire.
LESTER LEVENSON

LAUGH YOUR WAY TO LOVE

Cheerfulness keeps up a kind of daylight in the mind,
and fills it with a steady and perpetual serenity.
JOSEPH ADDISON

I have spoken of love many times in this book but what I would now like to emphasise is the importance of humour as a path to it. **Laughter is the path to love.** Love is a state of being, it is not simply an emotion that you occasionally experience, in fact it isn't an emotion at all, it is what you are. You are love, you are pure consciousness. The universal consciousness which I have spoken about throughout this book *is love.* If you don't feel that you are love, this only shows that there are blocks - there are clouds in the way preventing it from shining through.

Just as the sun is always shining,
even on a cloudy day,
so to is your love always shining,
but sometimes the clouds get in the way.

Please think carefully about the analogy between the shining sun and ourselves as shining love, because I believe the analogy is a good one.

Above the clouds there is always sunshine.
PROVERB

141

Picture the human being as an extremely luminous, radiating source of energy - and this energy is love. But we are generally not aware of this radiant love because it is almost constantly cloudy - these are the clouds that smoother our soul.

And how do we dispel the clouds of our soul? The great sage, the Maharishi Nolan John, says that the greatest tool that we have at our disposal, to dispel all fear and negativity and dispel the clouds, is laughter.

> *Humour is the solvent which*
> *dissolves the cloud of seriousness*
> *to reveal the radiance of the love ever present.*
> *NOLAN JOHN*

Seriousness is one of the major cloud thickeners and this can easily be dispelled by developing a sense of humour and having a really good laugh every day.

Master Nolan goes on to say that we shouldn't be asking "What is the meaning of life?", we should be asking "What is the meaning of laugh?", and instead of asking "Is there life elsewhere in the universe?" we should ask:

> *Is there laugh elsewhere in the Funiverse?*
> *NOLAN JOHN*

Laughter is not a learnt activity, it is a totally instinctive universal phenomenon. You can't translate a laugh as it is the same all over the world - every nationality, every culture, every race, every creed, every society, engages in this wonderful, but inexplicable activity. Apart from the spiritual benefits of laughter, there are obviously enormous physical benefits too. Laughter always results in an increased activity of the lungs and hence stimulates the flow of oxygen through the bloodstream, and, in addition, many of the body's internal organs are stimulated during laughter.

Laughter is the best medicine.
PROVERB

During a good session of laughter the body releases endorphins, the body's natural pain killers, and so can help to relieve physical pain. A good laugh leaves us feeling more physically alert, mentally sharper and, of course, in a much better emotional state. Research shows that laughter can also help to reduce high blood pressure. It has been shown repeatedly that laughter can actually cure illnesses, it speeds up the healing process and helps the natural, harmonious flow of energy through the body.

Studies have also shown that the health of people with a good sense of humour is significantly better than those who never laugh, and it is now well-known that successful people tend to have a better sense of humour than unsuccessful people. In my experience I have very rarely met successful, grumpy people - it is possible to be serious, grumpy and very rich - but this type of person is usually fairly miserable and therefore not successful in the true meaning of the word. One quality that all the most successful, healthy, happy people share is a good sense of humour.

Do not take life too seriously.
You will never get out of it alive.
ELBERT HUBBARD

Having a sense of humour somehow reflects our feeling about life and about ourselves. Those who laugh a lot have a way of looking at the world which enhances their general well-being, making them feel happier about life and more in harmony with themselves. A good laugh shared between friends releases tension, builds rappour, produces a relaxed atmosphere and brings forth the presence of love. Partners who laugh together are much more likely to stay together as the laughter somehow helps to dissipate many negative emotions such as anger, resentment and sorrow, and also enhances the bond between the couple.

Smiling is also very beneficial, but without the physiological advantages that laughing offers. If we smile a lot, apart from having a positive effect on those around us, it can also change the way that we are feeling. For many, a big smile is an excellent way to begin to overcome depression.

*A smile enriches those who receive it,
without making poorer those who give it..........
A smile brings rest to the weary, cheer to the discouraged,
sunshine to the sad, and is nature's best antidote for trouble.*
ANONYMOUS

A FINAL WORD

So, you are a being of infinite potential - you are God. We are all one. If you are unaware of this it is because your soul is residing in a poisoned body. Poisoned by toxic foods, seriousness, fear, resentment, and other negative emotions.

The blocks which stop us connecting to our higher self and realising our oneness are the same blocks that produce ill-health. If we could remove *all* blocks we would not only become enlightened but we would also experience an extremely high level of health. This is a state where your thoughts flow freely, your energy flows freely and you are in a constant state of love. It also means to be totally free of all ailments. This state of perfect human health is sometimes referred to as "Paradise Health" or "Heavenly Health".

Is your goal to attain Enlightenment or is it to attain paradise health? I see "the state of enlightenment" and "paradise health" to be two words for the same thing. But I prefer to express my own personal goal as *"to achieve paradise health"* rather than *"to achieve enlightenment"* because to the average person it sounds a bit more down to earth. The reason that I am explaining this here is so that you are aware that each step you take towards greater levels of spirituality is a step towards higher levels of health. The journey involves making all of your interactions with life, loving ones - to have awareness in everything you do, say, eat and think.

The spiritual journey involves looking after both
your soul and the temple of your soul.

Your journey towards enlightenment can be enhanced considerably by a number of factors outlined in this book but out of all of these, by far, the most important piece of advice that I could give is to **let all of your interactions with the universe be motivated by love**.

Develop a loving state of being
and your life will become literally heaven on earth.

The highest feeling is the experience of unity with All That Is.
This is the great return to truth for which the soul yearns.
This is the feeling of perfect love.
......In highest truth. love is all there is, all there was,
and all there will ever be.
NEALE DONALD WALSCH

Love in the past is only a memory.
Love in the future is a fantasy.
Only here and now can we truly love.
THE BUDDHA

145

Bibliography

A guide for the advanced soul - Susan Hayward. Published by In-tune books.

The Tao of physics - Fritjof Capra. Published by Flamingo.

Ageless body, timeless mind - Deepak Chopra. Published by Rider 1993.

Life after life - Raymond A. Moody Jr. M.D. Published by Bantam books.

Staying on the path - Dr. Wayne W. Dyer. Published by Hay House, Inc.

The Celestine Prophecy, An adventure - James Redfield. Published by Bantam books.

The Celestine Prophecy, An experiential guide - James Redfield and Carol Adrienne. Published by Bantam books.

The purpose of your life - Carol Adrienne. Published by Thorsons.

Conversations with God - Neale Donald Walsch. Published by Hodder and Staughton.

Meditations with God - Neale Donald Walsch. Published by Hodder and Staughton.

God spoke to me - Eileen Caddy. Published by The Findhorn press.

Living in the Light - Shakti Gawain. Published by Eden Grove Editions.

The Prophet - Kahlil Gibran. Published by Penguin Arkana.

Soul Centred Education - Christopher Gilmore. Published by Dovetales. Tel - 01270 652 392.

The promise of a new day - Karen Casey and Martha Vanceburg. Published by Hazelden Meditation series.

You can't afford the luxury of a negative thought - John-Roger and Peter McWilliams. Published by Thorsons.

Spiritual Nutrition and The Rainbow Diet - Gabriel Cousens. Published by Cassandra Press.

The Life and Teachings of the masters of the far East - Baird T. Spalding. Published by Devorss Publications.

The Philosophy of Natural Therapeutics - Henry Lindlahr. Published by the C.W. Daniel Company.

The medicine way - Kenneth Meadows. Published by Element.

The Personal Growth Handbook - Liz Hodgkinson. Published by Piatkus books.

I am me I am free - David Icke. Published by Bridge of love.

The Healing Power Of Sex - Judith Sachs. Published by Prentice Hall (US only).

You can Heal your life - Louise L. Hay. Published by Eden Grove Editions.

What we may be - Piero Ferrucci. Published by Thorsons

Being Oneself - F. W. Whiting. Published by The school of meditation.

Handbook to higher consciousness - Ken Keyes Jr. Published by Loveline books.

Feel the fear and do it anyway - Susan Jeffers. Published by Arrow Books Limited.

End the struggle and dance with life - Susan Jeffers. Published by Coronet Books limited.

You can have it all - Arnold Patent. Published by Money Mastery Publishing, 1984.

The nature of personal reality - Jane Roberts. Published by Prentice Hall, Inc.

Photoreading - Paul Scheele. Published by Learning Strategies Corporation.

When you come to the end of this phase of your existence, the value of your life will be measured not by how much you have accumulated, but by how much you have given away.

About the author

Tycho graduated from university in 1982 with a B.Sc. degree in Physics and Astrophysics. He then went on to become a professional musician and teacher of Guitar, Piano and Bass. In 1988 he obtained an Open University degree in Mathematics and Science and has since lectured at numerous colleges on a number of subjects.

After finishing his first degree in 1982 he set off around Europe on a personal pilgrimage that was to become the inspirational springboard for this series of books. During his time abroad, and since, he has extensively studied eastern philosophy including Yoga, Buddhism, and Martial arts comparing the principles of Eastern and Western religions and the various interpretations of the concept of God. His disattachment to any religion or doctrine has given him the scope to freely move among the various teachings with an open but necessarily doubting mind.

His path has led him to seek the universal roots of spirituality, extracting the essence of the many aspects of philosophical teachings and religions in the firm knowledge that each has its own treasures to uncover. His discoveries have led him primarily to acknowledge the relationships between the spirit, the mind, and the body working together in order to reach the highest quality of life.

Tycho's background was based on good conventional family values with encouragement towards individual self-discovery. These foundations created in the author a dual loyalty - a respect for established beliefs, both past and present, and an adventurous spirit, exploring new territory, questioning and probing the fertile terrain of life's secret gardens.

Andrea Photiou.

The Eureka Centre for Wholistic Health and Increasing Awareness

Tycho is currently running *The Eureka Centre for Wholistic Health and Increasing Awareness* situated in North London, which offers various courses and workshops designed for attaining high level health and enhancing your personal growth and spiritual development.

Tycho offers both private consultations and runs courses and workshops aimed at educating the public on the principles of Traditional Naturopathy and the factors that create perfect health. He also runs Healing Retreats in a Beautiful remote part of Tenerife in the Canary Islands.

The following is a popular 2 weekend course that Tycho runs in London, Manchester and at various other venues around the country:

ATTAINING HIGH LEVEL HEALTH

When health is absent wisdom cannot reveal itself;
art cannot manifest, strength cannot fight,
wealth becomes useless, and intelligence cannot be applied.
HEROPHILUS

This course teaches the essential principles of *traditional* naturopathy which are based on the idea that all healing is brought about by nature itself and not by the intervention of a doctor. Only nature can heal - but most of the time we not only don't allow it to, but we actual impede it by suppressing its natural healing ability. All we need to do to attain the high level of health that is the birth-right of every human being is:

1) Develop a state of being which aids the free flow of energy through the body - in practical terms this means to love life and to have a positive attitude towards all your experiences.
2) To give the body the *natural* resources in order to enable it to do its work; these are primarily fresh air, sunshine, exercise and natural raw foods.

This course will deal with these and other aspects of what creates high level health.

> *The disease ceases without the use of any kind of medicine, if only a proper way of living is adopted.*
> *AETIOS*

COURSE SYLLABUS

The basics of naturopathy; The cause of all illnesses; The cause of low level health; Vital energy, chi, prana, etc; Acute and Chronic illnesses; Eliminatory channels; The problems with suppression by drugs; Do the pharmaceutical companies really want a healthy society? Incurable diseases versus incurable patients.

The health potential of the human being; My health scale; Psychological, emotional, spiritual and physical factors; The basics of correct living; The dangers of indulgence; The importance of diet; Relaxation and meditation; Sunlight, fresh air, exercise and love.

A reassessment of the germ theory; Is there such a thing as a virus; Does HIV cause AIDS? An alternative theory of contagion; The theory of resonance.

The perfect diet for man; The Hay diet; Acidity and alkalinity; Fruit Versus greens; Nuts and seeds; Cooked versus Raw; Cows milk; Foods to definitely avoid.

A closer look at fasting; The problems caused by eating when ill; The dangers of vaccinations, mercury fillings; fluoride, detergents, anti-perspirants, etc.

A brief look at various healing modalities - oxygen therapy, energy medicine, colon detoxification, massage and Hydrotherapy; The benefits of cold air and water; The lymphatic system.

Death begins in the colon; Mucoid faecal matter; The dangers of bakery products; Auto-intoxication; The effect of laxatives; Enemas versus colonic irrigation; Colon cleansing; The intestinal flora.

The cholesterol myth; The cause of high blood pressure; The Great Calorie myth; Problems of a high carbohydrate diet; The cause and cure for diabetes; Osteoporosis and the calcium enigma.

The importance of relaxation, meditation and sleep; Various meditation techniques; Self-suggestion and Positive visualisation; Challenging the mechanistic world view; The power of consciousness; The power of love; The Aura; The Chakra system;

If you would like to enrol on this course, or for more information please phone:

(020) 8350 9600

OTHER BOOKS BY TYCHO PHOTIOU:

You Are What You Think - ISBN 1 902422 00 7
You Really Are Responsible - ISBN 1 902422 02 3
Inspirational Thoughts Vol. One - ISBN 1 902422 01 5
Inspirational Thoughts Vol. Two - ISBN 1 902422 03 1